||| || | || ||||||||||| ||| ||| ||| |||
D1600458

University of Winnipeg, 515 Portage Ave., Winnipeg, Manitoba, Canada R3B 2E9

T.S. ELIOT, VEDANTA AND BUDDHISM

PR
6009
. L43Z8697
1985

T.S. ELIOT, VEDANTA AND BUDDHISM

P.S. Sri

UNIVERSITY OF BRITISH COLUMBIA PRESS
VANCOUVER
1985

T.S. ELIOT, VEDANTA AND BUDDHISM

© The University of British Columbia Press 1985
All rights reserved

This book has been published with the help of a grant from the Canada Council and a grant from the Canadian Federation for the Humanities, using funds provided by the Social Sciences and Humanities Research Council of Canada.

Canadian Cataloguing in Publication Data

Sri, P.S., 1945-
   T.S.Eliot, Vedanta and Buddhism

Includes index.
Bibliography: p. 137
ISBN 0-7748-0239-1

1. Eliot, T.S., 1888-1965 - Philosophy.
2. Vedanta in literature. 3. Buddhism in
literature. I. Title.
PS3509.L43Z88 1985   821.912   C85-091470-1

International Standard Book Number 0-7748-0239-1

Printed and bound in Canada by John Deyell Company

To
Mother Teresa
who believes in doing small things with great love

CONTENTS

PREFACE

The influence of the Indian philosophical systems of Vedanta and Buddhism on the poetry and drama of T.S. Eliot is an important subject which deserves to be explored in detail.

I undertook this exploration six years ago in my doctoral dissertation, which I submitted to the Department of Comparative Literature of the University of Alberta and defended successfully in May 1979. Four years later, I forwarded the revised manuscript to the Canadian Federation for the Humanities. I was overjoyed when the Federation awarded me a subvention in May 1984. I was even more deeply gratified eight months later when the University of British Columbia Press agreed to publish my manuscript.

My study is a labour of love, meant to broaden our understanding of the literary and philosophical relations between the East and the West. By juxtaposing the essential perceptions of Indian philosophy with those of Eliot's poetry and drama, I have gauged the deep influence of Vedanta and Buddhism on his vision of the human condition. I have also demonstrated through precise quotation from Eliot's poems and plays that he has evoked the discrepancy between appearance and reality—a perennial theme in the literatures and philosophies of the East as well as of the West—with great intensity to sharpen our perception and to deepen our understanding of the turning world and the still point.

In exploring Eliot's ethos, I have taken into account the impact of Christian, Greek, and Latin authors on his works. However, his Christian outlook and classical leanings are both beyond question; they are already so well charted that it would have been superfluous for me to cover the same ground. I have focused, therefore, on Eliot's overt and covert use of Indian philosophical themes and symbols, with the sole aim of providing some fresh insights into Eliot's poetry and drama and of highlighting yet another dimension of his worldview.

I have refrained from the overuse of Sanskrit terms in my study to avoid mystifying my readers; instead, I have employed English equivalents wherever possible.

I acknowledge the financial assistance and research facilities extended to me by the University of Alberta. I am profoundly grateful to Norman Page and Robert J. Merrett for their friendly encouragement and invaluable advice. I am deeply indebted to Henry H. Kreisel for his abiding faith in me and my study. I thank A.H. Qureshi for supervising my thesis, Stephen H. Arnold and Milan V. Dimic for their sustained interest in my project, Jane C. Fredeman, Managing Editor of the University of British Columbia Press, for her unfailing courtesy and consideration, Jean Wilson for her excellent editorial services, Ms. Linda Pasmore for her meticulous typing of the manuscript, my family and friends for their moral support. Above all, I appreciate my wife, Jagada, for her love, loyalty, and devotion.

P.S.S.

ABBREVIATIONS

The following texts are frequently quoted in the book. Subsequent references to these texts are made in the abbreviated form shown on the left. The texts may all be found in *The Complete Poems and Plays of T.S. Eliot* (London: Faber and Faber, 1969).

A	"Animula"
AG	"At Graduation 1905"
AW	*Ash Wednesday*
BN	"Burnt Norton"
CC	*The Confidential Clerk*
CN	"Cousin Nancy"
CP	"Circe's Palace"
CP	*The Cocktail Party*
CR	*Choruses from "The Rock"*
DR	"Dans le Restaurant"
DS	"The Dry Salvages"
EC	"East Coker"
ES	*The Elder Statesman*
FA	"Fragment of an Agon"
FR	*The Family Reunion*
G	"Gerontion"
HM	*The Hollow Men*
JM	"Journey of the Magi"
LG	"Little Gidding"
LP	"The Love Song of J. Alfred Prufrock"
MA	"Mr. Appollinax"
MC	*Murder in the Cathedral*

P	"Preludes"
PL	"Portrait of a Lady"
RWN	"Rhapsody on a Windy Night"
SAN	"Sweeney Among the Nightingales"
SA	"Sweeney Agonistes"
SE	"Sweeney Erect"
WI	"Whispers of Immortality"
WL	*The Waste Land*

INTRODUCTION

The West is passing through a new Renaissance due to the sudden entry into its consciousness of a whole new world of ideas, shapes, and fancies. Even as its consciousness was enlarged in the period of the Renaissance by the revelation of the classical culture of Greece and Rome, there is a sudden growth of the spirit today effected by the new inheritance of Asia with which India is linked up. For the first time in the history of mankind, the consciousness of the unity of the world has dawned on us. Whether we like it or not, East and West have come together and can no more part.

S. RADHAKRISHNAN

The explication of the works of T.S. Eliot has now become a major enterprise. But the Indian philosophical themes and symbols which are fused with the Christian doctrine in his poetry and drama have not been scrutinized with the care and attention they deserve.

In *T.S. Eliot: A Symposium for His Sixtieth Birthday,* compiled by Richard March and Tambimuttu, only two of the forty-seven well-known poets and critics touch on the Indian side of Eliot. Montgomery Belgion, in "Irving Babbitt and the Continent," observes that the Buddhism of *The Waste Land* might have come from Babbitt, but he fails to develop his thesis.[1] E.F.C. Ludowyk suggests in "T.S. Eliot in Ceylon" that Eliot's readiness "to see the object not as it is, but in its symbolic setting, would appeal to readers to whom the idea of Maya is familiar," but he does not elaborate.[2] In *T.S. Eliot: A Study of His Writings by Several Hands,* edited by B. Rajan, Philip Wheelwright alone seems sensitive to Eliot's use of Eastern philosophy in his poetry, but his comments are brief and invite further study.[3]

Books on Eliot are either broadly suggestive or uncompromisingly sceptical of his use of Indian philosophy. Thus, both F.O. Matthiessen and Helen Gardner, in their otherwise admirable works on Eliot, tend to slight the Indian philosophical ideas in his poetry. Matthiessen nonchalantly declares that he has "not yet read the Upanishad from which Elliot borrowed" in *The Waste Land* and then makes the startling claim that in order to understand the poem it is unnecessary to read either the Buddha's Fire Sermon or the particular Upanishad from which Eliot borrowed.[4] Unquestionably, Eliot's poems stand on their own feet, but this does not entitle a scholar of Matthiessen's stature to rule out the significance of works he himself has not read. Gardner too is clearly upset by the introduction of Krishna in the third movement of "The Dry Salvages" and considers it an error.[5] Elizabeth Drew is more sympathetic to Eliot's absorption of "a great deal of Asiatic religion and philosophy" in *T.S. Eliot: The Design of His Poetry,* but she is too broad in her approach to analyse Eliot's orientalism in any great detail. Also, she does not seem to be especially familiar with either Buddhism or Hinduism.[6]

A few pioneering efforts have been made by some critics to evaluate the role played by Indian philosophical thought in Eliot's poetic development. At their best, however, these efforts are the outcome of partial understanding. Kristian Smidt, in his meticulous *Poetry and Belief in T.S. Eliot*, devotes part of a chapter to the discussion of "oriental mysticism" in Eliot, but he does not seriously attempt to relate it to Eliot's vision of the human condition.[7] Staffan Bergsten, in his fascinating *Time and Eternity*, is more interested in the oriental symbols adapted by Eliot than in the philosophical themes.[8] Herbert Howarth, in his informative *Notes on Some Figures behind T.S. Eliot*, describes Eliot's excursions into Indian philosophy and poetry with great enthusiasm, but he merely hints at their possible effect on his poetry and drama.[9] Harold McCarthy is persuasive when he points out that the "noble truths" of Buddhism are discernible in *Four Quartets*, but he does not satisfactorily explain why he omits a detailed discussion of the *Gita* (from which Eliot quotes) from his essay; nor does he attempt to reconcile the Buddhist ideas in the *Quartets* with Eliot's Christianity and his use of the *Gita.*[10] Narsingh Srivastava is at the other extreme in his exploration of the ideas of the *Gita* in the *Quartets,* for he takes no account of the Buddhist themes and makes no attempt to relate them to Eliot's use of the *Gita.*[11] Baird Shuman's article on the Buddhist influence in *The Cocktail Party* is well documented, but it suffers from mis-interpretation owing to Shuman's imperfect knowledge of Buddhist doctrine.[12] Rajnath is more interested in comparing the responses of Whitman and Eliot to the *Gita* than in assessing the influence of Indian philosophical systems on Eliot's works.[13]

Among the books written by Indians on Eliot, A.G. George's *T.S. Eliot: His Mind and Art* and B. Rajan's *The Overwhelming Question* are well known. But George's stress is on the existential themes in Eliot,[14] while Rajan is eloquent on what he calls "the poetry of failure" in Eliot.[15] Hence, both works have little to say about Indian philosophical influences on the poetry and drama of Eliot.

F.M. Ishak, in *The Mystical Philosophy of T.S. Eliot,* makes an ambitious attempt to elucidate the mystical connotations of the poems of Eliot and to trace the philosophical and literary influences that contributed to his 'mysticism.' The book provides some lucid and refreshing insights into Eliot's poetry and draws on both Eastern and Western mystical philosophy, but it does not clearly bring out the basic perceptions of the poetry of Eliot. The book is, moreover, limited in its scope; it confines itself to Eliot's poems, leaving out his plays. It falls short, therefore, of a complete examination of East-West ideosynthesis in Eliot's works and of his assessment of the human condition.

Amarnath Dwivedi's *Indian Thought and Tradition in T.S. Eliot's Poetry* sets out to evaluate the Indian influences on Eliot's poetry. Dwivedi dwells painstakingly on the 'explicit' references to Indian philosophical thought in Eliot's poetry. He ventures far afield into Indian myths and wisdom literature in order to squeeze out the last drop of meaning from these few 'explicit' references. The attempt, though laudable, does violence to Eliot's poetic ethos, for it subtly undermines the East-West *rapprochement* in Eliot by giving insufficient emphasis to the Western, notably Christian, elements in his poetry. Dwivedi does not pay much attention to the 'implicit' use Eliot makes of Indian philosophical themes and symbols; for instance, he fails to note Eliot's use of Tantrism in *Four Quartets.* Moreover, he does not examine the influence of Indian philosophy on Eliot's plays. Nor does he attempt to reconcile the Hindu-Buddhist philosophical notions with the Christian doctrine in his poetry. Hence, his book does not give a fully rounded picture of Eliot's worldview.

G. Nageswara Rao's *The Epic of the Soul* is strictly limited to *Four Quartets.* According to Rao, adequate critical attention has not been paid to the radically new form of the *Quartets* as "the epic of the soul." Borrowing his critical terminology and perspective from Sri Aurobindo, he attempts to relate the *Quartets* to spiritual classics like *The Divine Comedy, Paradise Lost,* and *Savitri.* His focus, therefore, is not primarily on the intense perceptions that form the basis of Eliot's poetry and dramas. And though he acknowledges the influence of Hindu-Buddhist thought on Eliot, he does not discuss the Tantric elements in the *Quartets.*

In his short yet lucid monograph, *Beneath the Axle-Tree*, J. Birje-Patil's concern is to introduce Eliot to beginners and to aid them in understanding Eliot. Hence, he does not elaborate on the Indian philosophical themes and symbols in Eliot's poetry and dramas.

Two other works invite comment. Mohit Kumar Ray's *T.S. Eliot: Search for a Critical Credo* is not concerned with the influence of Indian thought and sensibility on Eliot's poetry and drama; it is rather an attempt to show how Eliot moved from a 'monistic' towards a 'pluralistic' position as a literary critic. K.S. Misra, in *The Plays of T.S. Eliot: A Critical Study*, focuses on Eliot the dramatist. He analyses the texts, characters, structure and versification of the plays and tries to assess the dramatist's success in realizing his aims. Hence, he does not concern himself with the Indian philosophical themes and symbols in Eliot's work or their relation to his worldview.

We are left, therefore, with the uneasy feeling that the Indian face of Eliot has not been quite captured and—more important—that no significant attempt has been made to relate it to his vision of the human condition.

It is possible to dismiss Eliot's adventures in Indian philosophy as mere exoticism. "Exoticism," according to Mario Praz, is the "sensual and artistic externalization" of a poet who "invests remote periods and distant countries with the vibration of his own senses and materializes them in his imagination."[16] It has no room in it for a *participation mystique*, the profoundly internal act of meditation. Hence, exoticism is not indispensable to a poet who merely indulges a yearning for sensuous delights foreign to his own environment; nor does it truly nourish his creative imagination. When exoticism takes an oriental turn in a poet, we might expect allusions to such curiosities as dates and pomegranates, cinnabar and lacquer and mists through which temple bells resound.[17] Such exoticism, however, is not evident in the mature Eliot. Herbert Howarth writes:

> Eliot has naturalized into English from the Indian literature and the Indian sensibility little, and perhaps nothing, that is decorative. He denied himself the saffron paste, the sesamum seed, the açoka blossom, all the touches of pleasure that the Hindu landscape justified but that would be obviously exotic in a Western poem; all with the exception of images *already* naturalized in the Western imagination and languages; the unfolding lotus in Burnt Norton, for example. Perhaps he was kindled not by images of indulgence but by the austere language of old hymns, prayers, runes, and that led him first to the burned coloration of
> >   Rock and no water and the sandy road
> and then to poetry almost without adjectives:
> >   REILLY: Let them build the hearth
> >   Under the protection of the stars.
> >   ALEX: Let them place a chair each side of it.
> >   JULIA: May the holy ones watch over the roof,
> >   May the moon herself influence the bed
> where he found the words right for exciting a modern theatre audience to the same feelings—feelings of chill and awe, when the flesh creeps in

the presence of the elemental and eternal—that the antique words and rhythms excited in him.[18]

The young Eliot was no doubt fascinated with the romantic images of the East evoked by Kipling's *Kim*. Eliot read Kipling as a boy and apparently his boyish enthusiasm for Kipling never waned, for he later described *Kim* as Kipling's "maturest work on India, and his greatest book."[19] Also, he commented on the impact Kipling's Indian characters had on him:

> In his Indian tales, it is on the whole the Indian characters who have the greater reality, because they are treated with the understanding of love . . . . it is Purun Bhagat, it is the four great Indian characters in *Kim* who are real: the Lama, Mahbub Ali, Hurree Chunder Mookerjee, and the wealthy widow from the North . . . . Kipling is of India . . . . He might almost be called the first citizen of India.[20]

This was high praise indeed from such a fastidious critic as Eliot, who later found fault even with Shakespeare's characterization of Hamlet. There was, in fact, something pathetic in the staunch defence Eliot put up for everything that seemed journalistic or objectionable in Kipling, including his racial complex. As early as 1919, he seriously discussed the merits of Kipling's verse.[21] In 1941, he wrote a long introduction to his own selection of Kipling's verse and claimed that "in speaking of Kipling, we are entitled to say '*great* verse.' "[22] He even defended Kipling against a charge of anti-Semitism made by Lionel Trilling.[23] Clearly, Eliot never lost his wide-eyed fascination with Kipling and his writings.

When Eliot became aware of the mystical and metaphysical aspects of India in his mature years, the Kiplingesque image of India submerged in his consciousness, though not entirely, for at opportune moments it continued to surface in his poetry. For example, in the fifth section of *The Waste Land*, there is a vivid description of a torrid landscape parched for water so that the very air seems to pant for rain:

> Here is no water but only rock
> Rock and no water and the sandy road
> The road winding above among the mountains
> Which are mountains of rock without water
> If there were water we should stop and drink
>
> . . . .
>
> There is not even silence among the mountains
> But *dry sterile thunder without rain*
>
> . . . .

If there were rock
And also water
A spring
A *pool* among the rock

. . . .

Ganga was sunken, and the limp leaves
Waited for rain, while the black clouds
Gathered far distant, over Himavant.
The *jungle* crouched, humped in silence.
Then *spoke the thunder* (*WL*, p.74; my emphasis)

In *The Second Jungle Book*, we read how the Rains failed and the Jungle stream ran dry so that the rock bottom began to show:

That spring the *mohwa* tree . . . never flowered . . . . inch by inch, the untempered heat crept into the heart of the *Jungle*, turning it yellow, brown, and at last black . . . the hidden *pools* sank down and caked over . . . .

And the heat went on and on, and sucked up all the moisture, till at last the main channel of the *Waingunga* was the only stream that carried a trickle of water between its dead banks . . . . a long, lean blue ridge of *rock* [showed] *dry in the very centre of the stream* . . . .

The thunder was rolling up and down the *dry, scarred hills,* but *it brought no rain*—only heat-lightning that flickered behind the ridges— . . . 'THAT was the voice he heard.' (my emphasis)[24]

We can clearly perceive how closely Eliot's poem follows the general tenor of Kipling's description and even distinctly echoes certain words in it. Characteristically, however, Eliot changes the borrowed words to suit his own purpose and incorporates them into his poem. Thus, for instance, the stream "Waingunga," which is a tributary of the Ganges (called "Ganga" in Indian myth), is transformed into the main river, "the hidden pools" and the "blue ridge of rock" are combined to form "a pool among the rock," and the "dry, scarred hills" are identified with the Himalayas and given a specific name, "Himavant, " drawn from Indian myth.

Such a close resemblance in the passages describing the lack of life-giving water cannot be sheer coincidence. Eliot seems to have genuinely admired Kipling, and he paid the master the sincerest tribute one creative artist could pay another—imitation.

The young Eliot was drawn to the 'exotic' Orient from yet another direction. Later in his life, he himself recalled clearly "the moment" when, around the age of fourteen, he happened to pick up a copy of FitzGerald's Omar and received "an almost overwhelming introduction to a new world of feeling."[25] He commented: "It was like a sudden conversion; the world appeared anew, painted with bright, delicious and painful colours. Thereupon I took the usual adolescent course with Byron, Shelley, Keats, Rossetti, Swinburne."[26] It is curious that Eliot's adolescent romanticism should have been nourished by his reading of a mid-Eastern poet in translation, but the native literary scene probably did not offer him much in the way of inspiration, as he later admitted:

> Whatever may have been the literary scene of America between the beginning of the century and the year 1914, it remains in my mind a complete blank ... there was no poet in either century who could have been of use to a beginner in 1908. The only recourse was to poetry of another age, and to poetry of another language.[27]

Apparently, FitzGerald's *Rubiayat*, despite its deviations from the original, had enough 'oriental' flavour in it not only to satisfy Eliot's craving for novelty, but also to open up new vistas of romantic poetry to his mind. No doubt, Eliot cast off the spell of romanticism in his later years and became classical in his taste, but there was enough of the 'romantic' alive in him to "still enjoy" FitzGerald's Omar, even when he did not hold "that rather smart and shallow view of life."[28] And occasionally, there is a suspicion of the delicate world of FitzGerald's Omar in Eliot's poetry. The Magus, journeying towards Bethlehem with his two companions, has a moment of nostalgia when he yearns for "The summer palaces on slopes, the terraces,/ And silken girls bringing sherbet" (JM, p.103).

Neville Braybrooke has drawn critical attention to Eliot's juvenalia. While attending Smith's Academy, St. Louis—Eliot was sixteen then—he wrote two stories: "A Tale of a Whale" and "The Man Who Was King." Both have an 'exotic' setting in the South Pacific. Why did Eliot choose this locale for his stories? Braybrooke provides a likely answer:

> Two years before when he was fourteen, and at a time when the contemporary poetry of the period meant nothing to him, he read the Rubiayat of Omar Khayyam. The effect of FitzGerald's translation on him was quite overwhelming; he later recalled: 'The world appeared anew painted with bright, delicious and painful colours.' Yet it was a distant eastern world, and by comparison with it the islands of Hawaii and Paumoto in the Pacific seemed much less remote and closer to St. Louis and New England background. So the exoticism of Omar's world, it would seem, he replaced with an exoticism of his own.[29]

Braybrooke noted, however, that Eliot did not let his imagination run riot in his new-found enthusiasm. Hence, economy and precision were the hall-marks of both stories.

The first story is a cross between Melvillean whalehunting and Stevensonian adventuring on the South Pacific. The whaling ship in the story gets becalmed off Tanzatatapoo Island—an early sign of Eliot's genius for inventing queer-sounding exotic names. A whale is sighted, the ship gives chase, and the harpooner, who tells the story, jumps into a boat and shoots his harpoon. The 'leviathan' hurls the boat and its crew high into the air, but all three of them, including the harpooner, land on the whale's back and proceed to camp out there comfortably, even to the extent of cooking the flying fish for food! Their only fear is that at any moment the monster may plunge into the deep. All these intriguing incidents have more than a touch of Sindbad of the *Arabian Nights* about them!

The second story bears the distinct impress of FitzGerald and Kipling. It is called "The Man Who Was King"—a distorted echo of the title of Kipling's "The Man Who Would Be King." It concerns Captain Jimmy Magruder, a retired mariner, who has a reputation for telling sea-stories. We are told that Magruder is very fond of one particular yarn; each time the old salt spins it, it is embellished with more and more "wonderful incidents."[30] Which of us has not laughed with Mowgli at the wily old villain of the Jungle Books, Buldeo, who constantly tells "wonderful tales," each time with "additions and inventions"?[31] Indeed, the "teller of tall tales" in Buldeo seems reincarnated in Old Magruder. In his favourite story, Magruder is washed ashore on the island of Matahiva after a shipwreck. The local king is just dead and the islanders take Magruder's white skin and his sudden arrival to be signs from above and make him their new ruler. He is royally equipped with a fishing boat, a "palace"—"the size of a large woodshed"—and a harem.[32] His life consists of bathing, feasting, drinking wine and making love—surely a life-style FitzGerald's Omar would have envied! But Magruder's kingly life is brief; he is forced to flee since he can do none of the remarkable feats of his predecessor—like breathing fire or performing the rope trick (was an Indian fakir the guru of the ex-ruler of Matahiva?)!

While attending Smith Academy, Eliot wrote some "romantic" poetry too. In a poem called "A Lyric" (which was resurrected by Richard March and Tambimuttu from the Smith Academy Record for a symposium honouring Eliot's sixtieth birthday), he speculated on the riddle of "time" and "space" in the exotic vein of Omar:

> If time and space as sages say
>   Are things which cannot be,
> The sun which does not feel decay

No greater is than we.
So why, Love, should we ever pray
To live a century?
The butterfly that lives a day
Has lived eternity.[33]

Significantly, the words "time" and "space" were capitalized in Eliot's original manuscript; their metaphysical implications were to preoccupy him for a long time to come. Thus, in "Little Gidding," he rephrases the philosophical conundrum of his early years in a much more sophisticated tone and manner, without the "romantic" overtones of his early verse:

The moment of the rose, and the moment of the yew tree
Are of equal duration. A people without history
Is not redeemed from time, for history is a pattern
Of timeless moments. (LG, p. 197)

Eliot's "romantic" fascination with things oriental lingered on during his undergraduate years at Harvard. He enrolled at the University in 1906, took his bachelor's degree in 1909, and went on to complete his M.A. in 1910. He was an unobtrusive figure as an undergraduate. According to his contemporary at Harvard, William Chase Greene, "he was recognized as able and witty; not influential, at the time, rather aloof and silent; I used to tell him he reminded me of a smiling Buddha."[34] His name was seldom in the public eye, and even when his occasional poems and prose pieces were printed in the Harvard *Advocate*, he seemed "a quiet and minor talent."[35] A poem called "Circe's Palace," which appeared on 25 November 1908, is particularly intriguing, however, for its oblique references to India in the last stanza:

Panthers rise from their lairs
In the forest which thickens below,
Along the garden stairs
The sluggish python lies;
The peacocks walk stately and slow. (CP, p. 598)

The imagery might almost belong to the romantic agony in its last phase. The "panthers," "the sluggish python," the strutting "peacocks," and "the forest which thickens below" are all pure Kipling. Who can ever forget Bagheera, the fierce panther, Kaa, the terrible python, or Mor, the vain peacock, of the Mowgli stories? From these 'exotic,' colourful and almost 'decadent' descriptions, the poem moves to a terse and concluding statement that arrests our attention by its plainness: *"And they look at us with the eyes/*

Of men whom we knew long ago" (CP, p. 598; my emphasis). A striking image enforcing the theme of *recognition*—one destined to recur in the mature Eliot—among the prickly pears of *The Hollow Men* and in the unreal cities of *The Waste Land.* It is noteworthy that the 'colourful' elements in the poem reside cheek by jowl with the 'austere' ones—an indication surely of the gradual transition in Eliot from a maker of 'exotic' verse into a 'philosophical' and even 'mystical' poet. Indeed, Eliot did veer away from the "exotic" East in his mature poetry and drama. The romantic strains of Omar Khayyam and the crowded bazaars of *Kim's* Anglo-India are worlds away from the stern admonitions of the Buddha in the Fire Sermon, the austere counsel of the *Brihad-āranyaka Upanishad,* and the metaphysical subtleties of the *Gita.*

By his own admission, Eliot preferred "poetry with a clear philosophical pattern," since it satisfied "more of his own needs." Among the poets whom he liked for this reason, he included the "Forest Philosophers" of India.[36] Evidently, he was more attracted by austerity than sensuousness when he borrowed from the East.

Temperamentally, moreover, Eliot was as much inclined to philosophy as poetry. Both figured prominently in his formal education. At Harvard, he studied Sanskrit and Pali for two years (1910-11), probably in order to acquaint himself with Indian philosophical texts in the original, for he later admitted that though he studied "the ancient Indian languages" and "read a little poetry," he was "chiefly interested at that time in philosophy."[37] According to Howarth,

> Eliot's success as a philosopher almost decoyed him from literature . . . .
> He served as an Assistant in Philosophy in the academic years 1912-13 and 1913-14. He figured in the transactions of the University's Philosophical Club and was its president for the years 1913-14 . . . . In the Spring of 1914 he decided to go to Germany to complete his training, as many leading American teachers of philosophy had done. The Harvard authorities, who regarded him as a potential light of their Department of Philosophy, planned to advance him rapidly when he came home.[38]

However, Eliot was not a philosopher in the conventional academic sense, intent on expounding his *Weltanschauung* systematically through logic; indeed, he often integrated logically irreconcilable elements in his poetry. Rather, he was a visionary, passionately seeking a unifying principle of the universe and striving to transcend the flux of time through a mystic union with a timeless reality.[39]

Now, the "Forest Philosophers" of India and their successors use the Sanskrit word *darśana* meaning sight or vision to denote philosophy. By their standards, a philosopher is not a mere "lover of wisdom" but a *rṣi*—a seer or visionary.[40] *Darśana,* moreover, often resulted in *kavitā* or poetry; thus, a *rṣi* frequently became a *kavi* too. The words *ṛṣi* and *kavi* were even used interchangeably to mean poet, sage, prophet, and visionary. Eliot could well be described, therefore, as a *ṛṣi* or *kavi* from the Indian point of view.

It is again only too easy to discourage an investigation of East-West ideosynthesis in Eliot by quoting Eliot himself. For, while admitting that he had spent two years "in the study of Sanskrit under Charles Lanman" (author of *A Sanskrit Reader* and editor of the Harvard Oriental Series) and one year "in the maze of Patanjali's metaphysics under the guidance of James Woods," Eliot maintained that this study left him in a state of "enlightened mystification."[41] What he meant by this clever and ironic statement is debatable. Unfortunately, it is highly quotable and can be effectively used to discourage a Vedantic-cum-Buddhistic approach to Eliot. Still, when we take the time and effort spent by Eliot in Indian studies into account, it is not unreasonable to conclude that his "enlightened mystification" was not the result of a casual reading of Sanskrit texts and a passing interest in Indian philosophy. Moreover, the qualifying adjective "enlightened" suggests that Eliot's adventures in Indian philosophic thought were not in vain, and that they were, in fact, quite positive in their outcome. Consequently, his grasp of Indian thought could not have been as tenuous as some critics believe.

It is difficult to estimate precisely how much Eliot benefited from his Indic studies at Harvard. However, the poet in Eliot has rendered the problem redundant. No matter where, when and why he acquired this knowledge of Indian philosophical literature, he retained, assimilated, and incorporated it in his works in a most fruitful manner. Certainly, his studies enhanced his interest in Indian philosophy.

As early as 1918, Eliot reviewed for *The Egoist* an obscure treatise on Indian philosophy called *Brahmadarsanam or Intuition of the Absolute* by Sri Ananda Acharya. The review, though short, reveals that Eliot was thoroughly at home with Indian philosophical systems, texts, and their Sanskrit terminology and that he felt confident enough to make some sharp critical comments. He wrote:

A good brief introduction to Indian philosophy is still much to seek. Such a work ought to be both historical and comparative. It ought to draw the line very clearly between the religious intuition, which the various schools of philosophy all assumed, and the interpretations, which are widely diverse; it ought to make quite clear to the Occidental mind the difference between the Vedas and the Upanishads, which are properly religious texts, and the earliest philosophical texts of the primitive Sankhya. There is, though native writers are apt to obscure the fact, as certainly a History of Indian Philosophy as of European; a history which can be traced in the dualistic Sankhya, for instance, from the cryptic early couplets through the commentary of Patanjali to the extraordinarily ingenious and elaborate thought of Vachaspati Misra and Vijnana Bhikshu. There is, moreover, extremely subtle and patient psychology in the later writers; and it should be the task of the interpreter to make this psychology plausible, to exhibit it as something more than an arbitrary and fatiguing system of classifications.[42] Eliot went on to criticize the author for not developing the historical perspective and for being too concerned "with refuting some of the European scholar's dates." He concluded, however, by commending the author and drawing attention to a technical subtlety:

> Sri Ananda devotes most attention to Vedanta; but it is good to get a book which discusses the Sankhya at all. It ought to be made clear that Prakriti (Pradhanam) is not equivalent to Matter, but sometimes is almost the sense-data of the Realists.[43]

It is refreshing to encounter in a Westerner such an easy familiarity with an abstruse subject. These comments have no trace of either condescension or confusion. Nor is there any ready classification of the entire gamut of Indian thought as monistic or any quick assumption that all Indian philosophical systems revolve around navel-gazing. Instead, knowledge is combined with critical insight. Apparently, Eliot had more than a nodding acquaintance with Indian philosophy, though he never claimed the whole-hearted enthusiasm of an Irving Babbitt for Buddhism or the technical expertise of a James Horton Woods in Patanjali's metaphysics.

Indeed, Eliot's chief difficulty seemed to be his sentimental reluctance to transcend cultural barriers:

> A good half of the effort of understanding what the Indian philosophers were after—and their subtleties make most of the great European philosophers look like school boys—lay in trying to erase from my mind all the categories and kinds of distinction common to European philosophers from the time of the Greeks. My previous and concomitant study of European philosophy was hardly better than an obstacle. And I came to the conclusion—seeing also that the influence of Brahmin and Buddhist thought on Europe, as in Schopenhauer, Hartmann and Deussen, had largely been through romantic misunderstanding—that my only hope of really penetrating to the heart of the mystery would lie in forgetting how to think and feel as an American or a European, which, for practical as well as sentimental reasons, I did not wish to do.[44]

Such frank scepticism about the significance and even the possibility of any East-West interpenetration seems to rule out the discovery of an East-West ideosynthesis in Eliot's poetry and drama. But Eliot's statement that he did not *wish* "to penetrate to the heart of the mystery" implies that he was capable of such a penetration; only his fear that his occidental personality would be destroyed seems to have barred the way. And we must remember that the "tale" alone should be trusted and the "teller" taken *cum grano salis.* We would be unwise, therefore, to assume that Eliot's critical theory and poetic practice agreed completely. Often, artistic achievement and critical speculation do not correspond. Criticism is a highly self-conscious activity, while poetry draws upon a vast store of subconscious impressions, memories, and intuitions. Moreover, as Eliot admitted, a poet may be influenced even by works and authors about whom he is not overtly enthusiastic or of whom he has no expert knowledge.[45] Eliot's readings in Hindu-Buddhist thought seem to have lodged deep in his consciousness and surfaced from time to time in his works. Also, in spite of his deprecation of East-West *rapprochement,* Eliot seems to have made the attempt, as he declared in no uncertain terms:

> In the literature of Asia is great poetry. There is also profound wisdom and some very difficult metaphysics .... Long ago, I studied the ancient Indian languages, and while I was chiefly interested at that time in philosophy, I read a little poetry too; and I know that my own poetry shows the influence of Indian thought and sensibility.[46]

In fact, his interest in Indian philosophy ran deep. He was much moved by Buddhist writings: "I am not a Buddhist, but some of the early Buddhist scriptures affect me as parts of the Old Testament."[47] He thought that the Buddha's Fire Sermon "corresponds in importance to the Sermon on the Mount,"[48] declared that "what we learn from Dante or *Bhagavad Gita* or any other religious poetry, is what it feels like to believe that religion,"[49] and described *The Bhagavad Gita* as "the next greatest philosophical poem to *The Divine Comedy* within my experience."[50] Also, he kept a copy of *The Twenty-eight Upanishads* in his personal library for ready reference.[51]

Nor is it difficult to illustrate the *explicit* use Eliot made of Indian philosophy in his poetry; to cite but one example, he brought St. Augustine and the Buddha together at the very core of *The Waste Land* and noted that "the collocation of these two representatives of eastern and western asceticism, as the culmination of the poem, is not an accident."[52] It was certainly the outcome of something far deeper than "romantic misunderstanding."

It is perhaps useful at this point to list all the direct references to Indian philosophical themes and symbols in Eliot's poetry and drama.

The third section of *The Waste Land* is entitled "The Fire Sermon" and specifically recalls the Buddha's Fire Sermon from the *Maha-vagga*. Eliot quotes the words of the Buddha ("Burning burning burning") and acknowledges his debt in his notes to *The Waste Land:*

> The complete text of the Buddha's Fire Sermon (which corresponds in importance to the Sermon on the Mount) from which these words are taken, will be found translated in the late Henry Clarke Warren's *Buddhism in Translation* (Harvard Oriental Series). Mr. Warren was one of the great pioneers of Buddhist studies in the Occident.[53]

The fifth section of *The Waste Land,* entitled "What the Thunder Said," makes an equally direct and incontrovertible appeal to the *Brihad-aranyaka Upanishad.* Eliot acknowledges this appeal in his notes:

> 'Datta, dayadhvam, damyata' (Give, sympathize, control). The fable of the meaning of the Thunder is found in the *Brihad-aranyaka Upanishad*, 5, I. A translation is found in Deussen's *Sechzig Upanishads des Veda*, p. 489.[54]

Also, he briefly annotates the last line of "What the Thunder Said": "Shantih. Repeated as here, a formal ending to an Upanishad. 'The Peace which passeth understanding' is our equivalent to this word."[55]

In "Burnt Norton," the first poem in *Four Quartets,* there is a specific allusion to the lotus flower, symbol of ultimate reality in Hindu-Buddhist thought: "And the lotus rose, quietly, quietly,/ The surface glittered out of heart of light" (BN, p. 172).

The entire third section of "The Dry Salvages," the third poem in *Four Quartets,* broadly echoes the teachings of Krishna in the *Gita.* At one point, Eliot incorporates an almost literal translation of verse 5, from Chapter 8 of the *Gita.* Quite characteristically, he adapts the borrowed words, taking those which appeal to his imagination, twisting them gently to meet his own needs, and weaving them into the texture of his poem:

> At the moment which is not of action or inaction
> You can receive this: "on whatever sphere of being
> The mind of a man may be intent
> At the time of death"—that is the one action
> (And the time of death is every moment)
> Which shall fructify in the lives of others:
> And do not think of the fruit of action. (DS, p. 188)

In Act II of *The Cocktail Party*, there is an exact reference to the "Mahaparinibbana-sutta" of the *Digha-nikaya*, a sacred text of Buddhism. It occurs in Sir Henry Harcourt-Reilly's advice to Edward and Lavinia: "Go in peace. And work out your salvation with diligence" (*CP*, p. 411). The statement recurs in Sir Henry's parting address to Celia: "Go in peace, my daughter,/ Work out your salvation with diligence" (*CP*, p. 420). Later, Sir Henry alludes to the statement a third time, when he discusses Celia's destiny with her Aunt Julia; "And when I say to one like her/ 'Work out your salvation with diligence,' I do not understand/ What I myself am saying" (*CP*, p. 421). The reference is to the death-bed exhortation of the Buddha: "Then the Blessed One addressed the Priests: 'And now, O priests, I take my leave of you; all the constituents of being are transitory; work out your salvation with diligence.' And this was the last word of the Tathagata."[56] Why does Eliot include a quotation from the "Mahaparinibbana-sutta" in *The Cocktail Party*? Surely he cannot just be showing off his acquaintance with Warren's *Buddhism in Translations*.

Unless we regard all these *explicit* references to Indian philosophy in Eliot's poetry and drama as mere windowdressing, we must understand them as indispensable parts of organic wholes, indicating a particularly valuable method of penetration which might uncover the *implicit* use Eliot made of Indian philosophical themes and symbols in his poetry and drama.

Creative penetration which does not strain a text or distort the author's intentions beyond recognition is notoriously difficult. It would be prudent, therefore, to frame certain rules of thumb to aid us in the interpretation of Eliot's poetry and drama in the light of Vedanta and Buddhism.[57]

Eliot was first and foremost a *kavi*, concerned with embodying his particular vision of experiential reality in the unique form of his poetry. In other words, he was a "philosophical poet" akin to Dante and Lucretius, whom he regarded not as "philosophers" but as "poets," those "who have presented us with the emotional and sense equivalent for a definite philosophical system constructed by a philosopher—even though they may sometimes take little liberties with the system."[58] Like Dante and Lucretius, Eliot too had "something to say which is not even necessarily implicit in the system, something which is also over and above the verbal beauty." In short, Eliot's poetry is never deliberately didactic, and it is vain to look for any systematic exposition of an Eastern or a Western worldview in it. Nor is it legitimate to take him to task for not always footnoting his *implicit* use of Eastern or Western mysticism.

This does not mean that Eliot's vision could be understood in isolation. Of no other poet could it be more truly said, *il n'abandonne rien en route*. Eliot wrote with the past in his bones. Consequently, his poetry incorporates many disparate elements under the banner of an all-embracing Christianity, so that ultimately they have to be understood within the Christian context.

It is fruitless to speculate whether Eliot's Christianity was affected by his excursions into the realm of the Indian *darśanas*. We are concerned only with the influence of Indian thought on Eliot's works, not on his personal beliefs. Since even the average non-Christian reader can appreciate *Ash Wednesday* or *Murder in the Cathedral* without being converted to Christianity, Eliot could obviously be moved by the Indian *darśanas* without sacrificing his personal faith. Many great poets have adopted an eclectic approach and borrowed appropriate images and ideas wherever they found them; Eliot was merely following in their footsteps.

It is also difficult to say whether Eliot would have been a better poet if he had not been exposed to Indian philosophy and literature. He might have been just as good a poet, though not such a complex one, but certainly an interesting facet of experience would have been missing from his poetry.

Poetry, religion and philosophy are quite doubtless distinct from each other and may have different purposes in theory; but, in practice, they often merge. Poetry, for example, may embody powerful feelings in a unique form and yet carry both religious and philosophical overtones. For, at their profoundest and sublimest, poetry, religion and philosophy spring out of certain intense perceptions which have a universal significance. These perceptions, though immediate, may have far-reaching consequences and give birth to profound visions with their own imaginative order. These visions may become complex religions, lofty philosophies, or elaborate worldviews; but as intensely experienced perceptions, they are poetry.

We may, therefore, penetrate the work of a philosophical poet or *kavi* like Eliot by way of the keen perceptions underlying his poetry. By comparing these perceptions with those of Hindu-Buddhist thought, we may not only perceive the deep influence of Vedanta and Buddhism on Eliot's *Weltanschauung*, but also gain some insight into his vision of the human condition.

I

IMPERMANENCE AND SUFFERING

Action is transitory, — a step, a blow,
The motion of a muscle, this way or that —
'Tis done, and in the after-vacancy
We wonder at ourselves like men betrayed:
Suffering is permanent, obscure and dark,
And shares the nature of infinity.
WILLIAM WORDSWORTH

The fundamental perceptions of Vedanta as well as of Buddhism are those of the impermanence (*anithya*) or ephemerality of all phenomena and of the universality of suffering (*dukkha*). These insights are, of course, universal. We find them in the Old Testament, particularly in *Ecclesiastes* and *Job*; in the New Testament, we find Christ and his disciples repeatedly urging men to give up the things of this world since they do not have a lasting value for the human soul. A chief characteristic of seventeenth century English literature — a main source of literary inspiration to Eliot — was its acute awareness of the transience of life and the tyranny of time. However, in Vedanta and Buddhism, impermanence and suffering are essential perceptions; they are the bedrock on which entire philosophical systems rest. They are, moreover, closely associated with metempsychosis.[1]

Impermanence, when fully grasped, is applicable to the perceiver as well as to the objects perceived; the seer and the seen are both ephemeral, so that individuality or ego is at best an illusion. Suffering, when fully understood, is found to be inseparable from existence in the world of phenomena.

Thus, the words of Krishna to Arjuna on the battlefield of Kurukshetra echo through the corridors of time: "From the world of the senses, Arjuna, comes heat and comes cold, and pleasure and pain. They come and they go; they are transient."[2] The same perception is even more emphatically re-echoed in the words of the Buddha:

> Whether Buddhas arise, O priests, or whether Buddhas do not arise, it remains a fact and the fixed and necessary constitution of being, that all its constituents are transitory.
> Whether Buddhas arise, O priests, or whether Buddhas do not arise, it remains a fact and the fixed and necessary constitution of being, that all its constituents are misery.
> Whether Buddhas arise, O priests, or whether Buddhas do not arise, it remains a fact and the fixed and necessary constitution of being, that all its elements are lacking in an Ego.[3]

Indeed, in Vedanta and Buddhism, the transitoriness of life is even identified with suffering, so that suffering and impermanence become complementary aspects of a single primary perception.[4] Christianity too is imbued with a tragic awareness of suffering and of the fleetingness of the things of the world. This awareness finds a despondent expression in Dante's "Catholic philosophy of disillusion," which consists in not expecting "more from *life* than it can give or more from *human* beings than they can give, to look to death for what life cannot give."[5]

No sensitive thinking person can avoid recognizing that this perception is rooted in everyday experience of the world, in which birth and death, growth and decay, hope and despair are repeated *ad infinitum* and combine to produce a spectacle of suffering in which nothing remains stable and everything is in a state of flux.[6] The very best experiences are ephemeral; the most exquisite moments are flawed and fragmentary. Even as we look on in wonder, the sunset fades, the lily droops and drops down to the dust.

In a little known article he wrote in 1928, E.M. Forster dealt interestingly with Eliot's early poetry and *The Waste Land*. He made a significant and perceptive comment on Eliot's philosophy of life:

> In respect to the horror that they find in life, men can be divided into three classes. In the first class are those who have not suffered often or acutely; in the second, those who have escaped through horror into a further vision; in the third, those who continue to suffer. Most of us belong to the first class, and to the elect outside it our comments must sound shallow; they may feel that we have no right to comment at all. The mystics, such as Dostoievsky and Blake, belong to the second class.

Mr. Eliot, their equal in sensitiveness, distinct from them in fate, belongs to the third.[7]

Forster spoke more truly than he realized, for the notion of impermanence and suffering haunts much of Eliot's poetry.

Eliot was aware of the evanescence of life as early as 1905, when he passed out of Smith Academy; in a sentimental poem he wrote to mark his graduation, he philosophizes:

> We go; like flitting faces in a dream;
> Out of thy care and tutelage we pass
> Into the unknown world—class after class,
> O queen of schools—a momentary gleam,
> A bubble on the surface of the stream,
> A drop of dew on the morning grass. (AG, p. 594)

This vague disquiet over 'the passing show' reappears twelve years later in "The Lovesong of J. Alfred Prufrock" with an ironic overtone and a sharper outline; the hazy feeling of Eliot's youth has crystallized into a deep anxiety over the meaningless flux of life in which there are no stable and reassuring landmarks: "For I have known them all already, known them all—/ Have known the evenings, mornings, afternoons,/ I have measured out my life with coffee spoons" (LP, p. 14). Events repeat themselves endlessly so that the outcome is mere vacuity or boredom. Prufrock is acutely conscious of time passing and of his life slipping through his fingers without his ever daring to break free of his inhibitions and perceive the truth of his innermost self:

> There will be time, there will be time
> To prepare a face to meet the faces that you meet:
> There will be time to murder and create,
> And time for all the works and days of hands
> That lift and drop a question on your plate;
> Time for you and time for me,
> And time yet for a hundred indecisions,
> And for a hundred visions and revisions,
> Before the taking of a toast and tea. (LP, p. 14)

The very insistence of Prufrock's assertion betrays his inner uncertainties. He may try to persuade himself that there is time for him to make critical decisions which could transform his life, but ironically there will be no time; old age and death are inexorably creeping up on him. Prufrock is aware of this in his heart and is afraid, but he is unable to muster up his courage and ask "the overwhelming question":

> Should I, after tea and cakes and ices,
> Have the strength to force the moment to its crisis?
> But though I have wept and fasted, wept and prayed,
> Though I have seen my head (grown slightly bald)
>   brought in upon a platter,
> I am no prophet—and here's no great matter;
> I have seen the moment of my greatness flicker,
> And I have seen the eternal Footman hold my coat, and
>   snicker,
> And in short, I was afraid. (LP, p. 15)

Literally and metaphorically, he is enveloped in an ever-swirling fog in which the outlines of people and incidents are blurred and their features indistinct; he cannot relate to them meaningfully and so he is oppressed by loneliness and boredom. Unable to cope with the harsh realities of urban existence, he takes refuge in nightmarish fantasies or in futile daydreams. The images of his dreamworld—the "ragged claws," the "silent seas," and the singing mermaids—are all concrete and exact, in sharp contrast to the flowing concourse of his day-to-day world. Consequently, he finds his dreamworld reassuring and would fain linger "in the chambers of the sea/ By sea-girls wreathed with seaweed red and brown" (LP, p. 17), but it is impossible thus to escape the flux of existence, however meaningless it may be; and so Prufrock is compelled by human voices to wake up from his dreams. His is the tragedy of one so swept away by the flow of events in time that he cannot find even a momentary stay against confusion, the tragedy of Everyman who is tormented by suffering in its most refined and horrible form—ennui.

The poems which follow "Prufrock" exude the same foggy atmosphere of meaninglessness and futility; they depict in ironic and epigrammatic terseness the little anxieties, social embarrassments, and unacknowledged vacuities of polite society in Boston and London. It is a world in which frustrated society ladies indulge in casual affairs and sigh over lives without meaning, in which corrupt financiers and degenerate nobility drive hard bargains, but in the final reckoning find that they too have measured out their lives with coffee spoons. Cousin Nancy trying out "all the modern dances" (CN, p. 30), Burbank with his Baedeker and Bleistein with his cigar, Apeneck Sweeney laughingly indifferent to the song of the nightingales, Grishkin whose "friendly bust/ Gives promise of pneumatic bliss" (WI, p. 52)—apparently, their social lives are rich and satisfying; actually, they are boring, meaningless and futile, like peals of laughter trailing off into wails and ending in sobs. The desolation and murkiness of the urban landscape, the tenacity of the past from which the present cannot escape, the juxtaposition of the commonplace and the horrible, the breakdown in human relationships—all evoke a limbo in which nothing worthwhile can be done or experienced. The future seems bleak, the past is irredeemable, and the present is unbearable. So, one echoes Baudelaire: "What, in Heaven's name, has this world henceforth to do? . . . Progress has atrophied in us all that is spiritual . . . and there cannot be any progress (true progress, that is to say, moral progress) except within the individual himself."[8] Or, like Gerontion, one contemplates the endlessly shifting scene with horror and despair and awaits death.

"Prufrock" exemplifies the tragicomedy of a middle-aged man, with "a bald spot" in his hair and a romantic disposition, who retreats into his dreamworld to escape his futile existence; his "mermaids" are the opium that relieves his ennui. "Gerontion," on the other hand, represents the tragedy of a thoroughly disillusioned old man who has no faith to sustain him and nothing to look forward to except death. He sees too clearly to take refuge in dreams. Consequently, he has only the "thoughts of a dry brain in a dry season" (G, p. 39). He is an intellectual with a keen sense of history and a knowledge of international affairs who has moved freely in a cosmopolitan world of finance and corruption. He has eschewed that ultimate modern evil, war, and apparently led a rich and blameless life. Still, he is tormented by guilt, for in his pursuit of sensual and intellectual gratification, he has forsaken the spiritual, personified as Christ the tiger. Towards the end of his life, he discovers that the people and events he has assiduously courted are all fleeting, merely part of a gyrating, whirling flux of existence, incapable of affording him any permanent satisfaction and happiness: "Vacant shuttles/ Weave the wind" (G, p. 38). He has not even the "ghosts" of his former life, memories, to live on. His youth is fled and his house decayed so that he faces an empty old age and death. He can find no intellectual solution to his predicament, since it is essentially one of spiritual distress. His lifelong pursuit of truth as an intellectual abstraction has been in vain, and his extensive knowledge of human events is of no avail, for history cannot furnish him with wisdom or perception of the ultimate truth: "History has many cunning passages, contrived corridors/ And issues, deceives with whispering ambitions,/ Guides us by vanities" (G, p. 38). In short, Gerontion learns to his dismay that his rational and humanistic attitude towards life will not save him. His is the tragic lot of a man who has found such a good servant in reason that he has become its enamoured slave. He suffers not from an undeveloped mind or heart, but from an undeveloped soul. Only a logic-transcending faith in a divinity that shapes our ends can liberate him from such suffering. So, he perches outside his decayed house, contemplating the ruinous whirligig of life without and within, and waits for the rain of divine grace to moisten his parched soul. But that kind of rain will come only after the emptiness of the Waste Land is behind the seeker and a full measure of suffering has scorched and purified his soul.

In the poems Eliot published before *The Waste Land*, suffering is identified with loneliness, frustration and impotence, so that there is the heart-searing lament over the meaninglessness of life spent amidst the fog and smoke of winter afternoons. With the publication of *The Waste Land* in 1922, the perception of suffering becomes deeper so that it is seen to be universal, prevalent in the lives of the ancients as well as the moderns, among the heroes and saints of yore as well as among the typists and clerks of the contemporary world.

It is commonly held that Eliot criticizes our materialistic civilization and our loss of spiritual values by evoking the squalor, emptiness, and meaninglessness of modern life.[9] Eliot himself, however, reacted sharply to this view that 'dates' his poems and confines his ideas to a particular epoch:

> I dislike the word generation. When I wrote a poem called *The Waste Land* some of the more approving critics said that I had expressed "the disillusionment of a generation," which is nonsense. I may have expressed for them their own illusion of being disillusioned, but that did not form part of my intention.[10]

Eliot's irritation is natural, for such criticism ignores the fact that the true poet writes for all time, while addressing himself to the deepest truths of his own time. The many languages, cultures, and experiences which Eliot incorporates in his poems, especially *The Waste Land*, testify to the universality of his concerns. In *The Waste Land*, the ancient and the modern often reside cheek by jowl, and the language at times teases us out of past, present, and future into the eternal. In short, Eliot's poetry concerns man, his civilization, and his destiny. Specifically, it deals with the perennial problem of human suffering and gropes for a positive way out of suffering to freedom.[11] Hence, Eliot is responding to the same fundamental perception that moved Krishna or the Buddha (or, for that matter, Christ) and embodying his responses in poetry. Seen in this light, *The Waste Land* becomes a poetic restatement of Eliot's speculation that "the deeper design" may be that "of human misery and bondage which is universal."[12]

The original epigraph to *The Waste Land*, which Eliot rejected on Pound's advice, is from Conrad's *Heart of Darkness*:

> Did he live his life again in every detail of desire, temptation and surrender during that supreme moment of complete knowledge? He cried in a whisper at some image, at some vision—he cried out twice, a cry that was no more than a breath—"The horror! The horror!"[13]

Kurtz is horrified because he lives his life all over again in his imagination. He is relieved when death finally arrives. His horror stems, therefore, from being enmeshed in continual suffering, in life without end.

The final epigraph to *The Waste Land* comes from Petronius' *Satyricon* and refers to the Cumaean Sibyl, the famous ancient Greek prophetess, whom Apollo granted a life of as many years as she had grains of dust in her hand. She forgot to ask, however, for eternal youth and so shrank away to nothing. She hung in a jar and when asked, "What do you want?" she replied, "I want to die." Here again is the horror of the inability to die and of the necessity to suffer endlessly.

Universal and endless suffering is also perceived by Tiresias who, according to Eliot, is the central uniting figure in the poem:

> . . . although a mere spectator and not indeed a "character," [Tiresias] is yet the most important personage in the poem, *uniting all the rest.* Just as the one-eyed merchant, seller of currants, melts into the Phoenecian sailor, and the latter is not wholly distinct from Ferdinand, Prince of Naples, so all women are one woman, and the two sexes meet in Tiresias. What Tiresias *sees*, in fact, is the substance of the poem. (*WL*, p. 218)

In other words, Tiresias is all the different characters in the poem; they are his own self reincarnated endlessly in different lives, which are yet one life, united in his consciousness.[14]

Commenting on Eliot's note on Tiresias, Stephen Spender remarked that it might induce the student of Eliot's poetry to conclude that "one-eyed merchant equals Phoenician sailor equals Ferdinand, Prince of Naples."[15] This is precisely Eliot's intention. He wants us to understand that suffering is universal, omnipresent, and endless in the phenomenal world; we have to repeat the cyclic process of birth, growth, decay, and death again and again and yet again. Only a Tiresias is aware of his previous lives; most of us are not, because we have not refined our consciousness to perceive them. The full horror of existence, the horror which Kurtz and the Sibyl dimly perceive, is mercifully concealed from the majority of mankind, for mankind cannot bear very much reality.

The Waste Land, then, *appears* to be a collection of dramatic monologues uttered by different voices, ancient and modern; *actually*, the poem is Tiresias remembering his past lives, *seeing* them all unroll before his mind's eye.[16] He is in much the same condition as Kurtz or the Sibyl, "throbbing between two lives" (*WL*, p. 68). Tiresias, therefore, is not impersonating these characters; he *is* these characters; he is seeing himself enacting different roles at different times and enduring the same suffering: "And I Tiresias have foresuffered all/ Enacted on the same divan or bed" (*WL*, p. 69). The characters range from queens to washerwomen, from warriors to clerks and from sinners to saints. The faces and lives may be different, but the underlying consciousness is the same. And sameness is bound to produce ennui, a most refined and horrible form of suffering.

The idea of reincarnation or metempsychosis is present in Vedanta as well as Buddhism. The individual consciousness evolves towards the freedom of total self-awareness or *nirvāṇa* through innumerable lives; in this evolution, the incarnations may be higher or lower in order. This idea, though not an article of faith, is implicit in Christianity, which urges the individual to repent his sins and to be reborn *in divinis*, as otherwise he will sink to perdition. Eliot reinforces the idea of reincarnation in *The Waste Land* by grafting on to it the myth of the Fisher-King, which concerns a land that has been laid waste by a curse and so produces neither vegetable nor animal life. The curse is removed when a knight appears in search of the Holy Grail and the land is resurrected. The resurrection of the waste land is also connected with primitive fertility cults, which

> conceived of the cycle of the seasons as the life of a god who controlled the energies of nature, and who nevertheless had to submit to the power of death. But the death of the god was not permanent, for it was followed by a resurrection . . . . And since water was the basic necessity of these agricultural communities, the resurrection of the god coincided with the coming of the spring rains, the central symbol of the fertilizing process . . . . But these early vegetation myths developed later into "the mystery religions," which linked the ideas of death and resurrection in the natural world with that of a parallel process in the world of the spirit.[17]

Eliot, in short, marries myth and metaphor to emphasize the philosophical notion of metempsychosis.[18]

In his notes to *The Waste Land*, Eliot acknowledges that he owed his ideas of fertility rites and the resurrection of the waste land to J.G. Frazer's *The Golden Bough* and Jessie Weston's *From Ritual to Romance:*

> Not only the title, but the plan and a good deal of the incidental symbolism of the poem was suggested by Miss Jessie L. Weston's book on the Grail legend: *From Ritual to Romance* (Cambridge). Indeed, so deeply am I indebted, Miss Weston's book elucidates the difficulties of the poem much better than my notes can do; and I recommend it (apart from the great interest of the book itself) to any who think such elucidation of the poem worth the trouble. To another work of anthropology I am indebted in general, one which has influenced our generation

profoundly; I mean *The Golden Bough*; I have used especially the two volumes *Adonis, Attis, Osiris*. Anyone who is acquainted with these works will immediately recognise in the poem certain references to vegetation ceremonies.[19]

Both Weston and Frazer hark back to oriental myths to describe the origin of fertility rites and the Grail legend.

Weston, for instance, draws attention to certain curious parallels between the Grail legend and the *Rig Veda* as well as the *Mahabharata*. In the *Rig Veda*, the god Indra releases the imprisoned waters just as Gawain and Perceval do in the Grail legend:

it is Indra to whom a disproportionate number of hymns of the *Rig Veda* are addressed . . . . it is from him the much desired boon of rain and abundant waters is besought, and that the feat which above all others redounded to his praise, and is ceaselessly glorified both by the god himself, and his grateful worshippers, is precisely the feat by which the Grail heroes, Gawain and Perceval, rejoiced the hearts of a suffering folk, i.e., the restoration of the rivers to their channels, the "Freeing of the Waters." Tradition relates that the seven great rivers of India had been imprisoned by the evil giant, Vritra, or Ahi, whom Indra slew, thereby releasing the streams from their captivity.[20]

In the *Mahabharata*, the story of Ṛṣyaśṛṅga bears a curious resemblance to that of Perceval:

the lonely upbringing of the youth in a forest, far from the haunts of men, his absolute ignorance of the existence of human beings other than his parent and himself, present a close parallel to the accounts of Perceval's youth and woodland life, as related in the Grail romances . . . . The circumstances under which Rishyaçringa is lured from his Hermitage are curiously paralleled by the account, from in the *Queste* and Manessier, of Perceval's temptation by a friend, in the form of a fair maiden, who comes to him by water in a vessel hung with black silk, and with great riches on board.[21]

Weston concludes that the specific task of the Grail hero was not a literary invention but an inheritance from Aryan tradition; the Grail story was, moreover, rooted in ancient ritual, "having for its ultimate object, the initiation into the secret sources of Life, physical and spiritual."[22]

The central personality of the Grail story, the Fisher-King, whose infirmity brings misfortune on his land, is also linked to Indian tradition, according to Weston. She poses a significant question—why should he be called the *Fisher*-King?—and answers it by an examination of the fish symbolism. She is aware that those who hold the Grail story to be fundamentally Christian have associated the fish symbolism with Christ and his disciples, whom he promised to make "Fishers of Men." She alleges, however, that Christianity "did no more than take over, and adapt to its own use, a symbolism already endowed with a deeply rooted prestige and importance."[23] She affirms that the fish is "a Life symbol of immemorial antiquity" and goes back to the Hindu and Buddhist mythologies to prove her point:

> In Indian cosmogony Manu finds a little fish in the water in which he would wash his hand; it asks, and receives, his protection, asserting that when grown to full size it will save Manu from the universal deluge. This is Jhasa, the greatest of all fish.
>
> The first Avatar of Vishnu the Creator is a Fish. At the great feast in honour of this god, held on twelfth day of the first month of the Indian year, Vishnu is represented under the form of a golden Fish.... The Fish Avatar was afterwards transferred to Buddha.
>
> In Buddhist religion, the symbols of the Fish and Fisher are freely employed. Thus in Buddhist monasteries we find drums and gongs in the shape of a fish, but the true meaning of the symbol, while still regarded as sacred, has been lost, and like the explanation of the Grail romances, are often fantastic afterthoughts.
>
> In the Mahayana scriptures, the Buddha is referred to as the Fisherman who draws fish from the ocean of Samsara to the light of Salvation. There are figures and pictures which represent Buddha in the act of fishing, an attitude which, unless interpreted in a symbolic sense, would be utterly at variance with the tenets of the Buddhist religion.[24]

These close parallels between oriental religions and Christianity are not accidental, according to Weston. They clearly indicate Christianity's Eastern origins and its retention of certain oriental symbols and practices even after its adaptation to the Western world. She quotes from Father Cumont's *Religions Orientales* to support her argument:

> Reasearches on the doctrines and practices common to Christianity and the Oriental Mysteries almost invariably go back, beyond the limits of the Roman Empire, to the Hellenized East. It is there we must seek the key of enigmas still unsolved. The essential fact to remember is that the Eastern religions had diffused, first anterior to, then parallel with, Christianity, doctrines which acquired with this latter a universal authority in the decline of the ancient world.[25]

The concepts and customs of the ancient world, in other words, have been reincarnated in a refined and modified form in Christianity—metempsychosis in operation on a conceptual plane.

Frazer too turns to oriental religions to explain the vegetation ceremonies. It is interesting to note, for instance, that he subtitles the two volumes of *The Golden Bough* which Eliot used especially as "Studies in the Histories of *Oriental* Religions" (my emphasis). Eliot devoted considerable time and effort to the study of oriental languages and scriptures. Could this have stimulated his interest in Frazer's application of anthropology to comparative religion? In an exhaustive study called *The Literary Impact of "The Golden Bough,"* John B. Vickery suggests that this was, in fact, the case:

> it is clear that Eliot possessed a well-developed and persistent interest in psychology and anthropology, particularly as they applied to comparative religion. Precisely when this interest was aroused is hard to say. It may have been during the years when Eliot was a Harvard undergraduate or a graduate studying philosophy and literature in Paris, that is, in the period from 1906 through 1911 . . . . a more likely date for Eliot's initial acquaintance with Frazer and Frazer-influenced works is from late 1911 or early 1912 through 1915. For one thing, a number of important studies of myth and ritual receiving their orientation from *The Golden Bough* . . . did not appear until 1912 or later. Coupled with this is the fact that from 1911 to 1915 Eliot was reading Sanskrit and philosophy at Harvard and in Europe. Both the subjects and his instructors, especially James Woods, could easily have intensified his familiarity with the Cambridge school, *The Golden Bough*, and comparative religion generally.[26]

Vickery points out that Frazer traces the origin of fertility rites and vegetation ceremonies associated with the death and resurrection of Adonis, Attis, and Osiris to ancient Indian rituals and that some of these rituals are still extant.[27] According to Vickery, Eliot extends the association further to the death and resurrection of Christ:

> the god's death is not, to the true believer, an irredeemable catastrophe and tragedy. As Frazer remarks in the chapter entitled "The Killing of the Tree Spirit," the death of the god is "merely a necessary step to his revival or resurrection in a better form. Far from being an extinction of the divine spirit, it is only the beginning of a purer and stronger manifestation of it." Historically, this is borne out by the first explicit appearance of Christ in "What the Thunder Said." After the Adonises, Attises and Osirises of the world he comes as the "stronger manifestation" of divinity, the Christian dying and reviving man-god.[28]

Christ, then, is an incarnation higher in the hierarchy than the other man-gods. The notion of a man-god regenerating the waste land may, therefore, be said to have evolved through Adonis, Attis, and Osiris towards Christ—metempsychosis at work on a metaphysical plane.

Frazer discusses the Sybil too. He finds a parallel to the Sybil legend in the folktale about a girl in London whose wish to live forever was granted. Eliot too connects the past with the present by showing that London contains its own contemporary Sybils, reincarnated in the persons of the anonymous lady of "A Game of Chess," Lil, and the typist. Each is faced with an endless vista of misery, despair, and boredom; each is a mute prophetess enduring the doom of the phenomenal world, unending life, and spiritual degradation.

The Sybil's concern with death is also elaborated in the opening section, "The Burial of the Dead," in terms of the life, death, and resurrection of vegetation:

> April is the cruellest month, breeding
> Lilacs out of the dead land, mixing
> Memory and desire, stirring
> Dull roots with spring rain. (*WL*, p.61)

The overwhelming feeling is of dread mixed with watchful anticipation. Why is April, the beginning of spring, called the "cruellest month"? Vikery has a plausible answer:

> ... to contemporary ears the attributing of cruelty to April is an arresting and somewhat puzzling idea. But stated most simply, the reason for describing April as the cruellest month is that it marks the point at which the vegetative and human cycles both intersect and contradict each other. Vegetation begins to bloom at the time of the crucifixion and death of Christ, the man-god. Inevitably in such a situation man's attitude is one of bewilderment and uncertainty, for he is compelled to face the complexities of his world. This feeling that April is a time of great crisis is also reflected in *The Golden Bough*'s discussion of a number of April rituals designed to protect people from the evil and destruction of the world. Coupled with this is April's connection with the burial ceremonies. The reference to the office of "The Burial of the Dead" reminds us that the death of Christ occurred in the spring . . . . In addition, festivals of mourning for the dead Adonis often took place in the spring. By these allusions implicit in April's cruelty, Eliot links Christ and Adonis to suggest that both their deaths were part of those ritual celebrations that protected man from the overwhelming power of evil. And since Adonis was a vegetative deity it is inevitable that his departure should be matched by a "dead land" filled only with "dull roots" and "dried tubers."[29]

April, then, seeks to awaken man and the world to her critical nature as well as to the death and burial of the man-god. This is why lilacs bloom and are vivified by rain; the lilacs are "a symbol not only of the miracle of birth in a dead land but of memory," enabling us to recall "the dying and reviving god, Attis, whose return from the dead was foreshadowed in the appearance of lilac-coloured blossoms at the very beginning of spring." The lilacs appear, moreover, along with the rain; together they symbolize "the revival and awakening of the human consciousness to its religious dimensions."[30] Myth and metaphor coalesce, therefore, in Eliot's poetic exploitation of the philosophical notion of metempsychosis and of the anthropological discoveries connected with the vegetation ceremonies.

Since metempsychosis involves endless reincarnations and these in turn result in ennui, ennui is how suffering manifests itself in the waste land. Ennui is the outcome of the feeling that there is nothing new, that birth, growth, decay, and death repeat themselves endlessly and that history is a meaningless cyclic process. Consequently, apathy and boredom pervade the lives of the ancients as well as the moderns in *The Waste Land* and are mirrored in the physical condition of the land:

> A heap of broken images, where the sun beats,
> And the dead tree gives no shelter, the cricket
>   no relief,
> And the dry stone no sound of water. (*WL*, p. 61)

> Here is no water but only rock
> Rock and no water and the sandy road (*WL*, p. 72)

The appalling emptiness of the inhabitants of this waste land is captured vividly in the words of the anonymous lady of "A Game of Chess":

> 'My nerves are bad tonight. Yes, bad. Stay with me.
> 'Speak to me, Why do you never speak. Speak.
> 'What are you thinking of? What thinking? What?
> 'I never know what you are thinking. Think.'
> . . . .
> 'What shall I do now? What shall I do?
> 'I shall rush out as I am, and walk the street
> 'With my hair down, so. What shall we do tomorrow?
> 'What shall we ever do?'
>   The hot water at ten.
> And if it rains, a closed car at four,
> And we shall play a game of chess,
> Pressing lidless eyes and waiting for a knock upon
>   the door. (*WL*, p. 65)

This is a condition of acute spiritual distress, terrifying in its meaninglessness.[31]

This spiritual distress or *Angst* so prevalent in *The Waste Land* spills over into *The Hollow Men*. The haunting rhythm hammers home the despair over life's incertitude and unending pain and laments the absence of a life-renewing force. In the world of the hollow men, the stuffed men, the shadow ever falls "Between the conception/ And the creation" (*HM*, p. 85), so that nothing ever happens and everything is in a state of limbo. In death's dream kingdom, a twilight world of inaction, there are only the debris of civilization and voices singing in the wind. Even the witness to this desolation is a pitiful scarecrow of a man, dressed in dead rats' coats and crows' skins to scare other rats and crows, caricaturing the emptiness in the lives of others like himself.

The desolation of this twilight world is underscored by the epigraphs. The first is from *Heart of Darkness*—"Mistuh Kurtz—he dead" (*HM*, p. 83)—a pronouncement that leaves Marlow unmoved in Conrad's tale for the 'horror' Kurtz has perceived, his vision of endless suffering, lives on in Marlow's memory. In fact, Kurtz's final words—"The horror! The horror!"—haunt Marlow and ring persistently in his ears, even during his brief visit a year later to Kurtz's "Intended," who continues to mourn his death. The second epigraph—"A Penny for the Old Guy" (*HM*, p. 83)—is even more significant. It recalls Guy Fawkes, that notorious Jacobean conspirator who was caught and executed before he could blow up the House of Commons, so that what should have ended with a big bang ended merely in a whimper. Since then, his death has been celebrated annually. The anarchist, in other words, has displaced the man-gods in the popular imagination: Adonis, Attis, Osiris and Christ have been supplanted by the Old Guy. Consequently, the world of the hollow men is a waste land in which there is not even a glimmer of hope for redemption:

> This is the dead land
> This is cactus land
> Here the stone images
> Are raised, here they receive
> The supplication of a dead man's hand
> Under the twinkle of a fading star. (*HM*, p. 84)

So, the hollow men go round and round the prickly pear, unable to undo their own past and be freed of their *karma* (the cumulative effect of their past deeds).[32] They can only live their lives over and over and endlessly endure the impermanence and suffering of the phenomenal world.

Ash Wednesday marks a turning point in Eliot's poetic vision. No longer does it survey a barren waste land; now, for the first time, there is water in the wilderness and anxiety is balanced by hope. The perception of transience and agony is offset by an awareness of the possibility of rising to a higher sphere of being. This awareness swells in *Four Quartets* to a positive and joyful affirmation of a transcendental reality. This does not mean, however, that impermanence and suffering lose their force amidst the hope and joy of the later poems. The greater the bliss, the sharper the agony of losing it.

Thus, the speaker in *Ash Wednesday* is acutely conscious of "the infirm glory of the positive hour" and of the limitations of the phenomenal world:

> Because I know that time is always time
> And place is always and only place
> And what is actual is actual only for one time
> And only for one place
> I rejoice that things are as they are. (*AW*, p. 89)

He has only a faint hope of liberation to sustain him in his long purgatorial climb from the depths of agony to the heights of ecstasy. His yearning to be free of incertitude and suffering and to find the peace that passes understanding bursts out:

> Where shall the word be found, where will the word
> Resound? Not here, there is not enough silence
> Not on the sea or on the islands, not
> On the mainland, in the desert or the rain land,
> For those who walk in darkness
> Both in the day time and in the night time
> The right time and the right place are not here. (*AW*, p. 96)

Tearfully, he implores "the veiled sister" (the Holy Virgin or Dante's Beatrice reincarnated?) to intercede for him and pray for all

> Those who walk in darkness, who chose thee and oppose thee,
> Those who are torn on the horn between season and season,
>   time and time, between
> Hour and hour, word and word, power and power, those who wait
> In darkness . . .
> . . . those who offend her
> And are terrified and cannot surrender
> And affirm the world and deny between the rocks
> In the last desert between the last blue rocks (*AW*, pp. 96-97)

We are back in the waste land, and the desert air resounds to cries of self-doubt, agony, and despair. But the darkness is not all-pervasive; "the veiled sister" *can* be seen and does provide a gleam of hope.

The spark brightens to a blaze in *Four Quartets*; and, paradoxically, the darkness seems more intense. Thus, the perception of transience, or of impermanence in the phenomenal world, is given profound poetical expression in the opening lines of "East Coker":

> In my beginning is my end. In succession
> Houses rise and fall, crumble, are extended,
> Are removed, destroyed, restored, or in their place
> Is an open field, or a factory, or a by-pass.
> Old stone to new building, old timber to new fires,
> Old fires to ashes, and ashes to the earth
> Which is already flesh, fur and faeces,
> Bone of man and beast, cornstalk and leaf.
> Houses live and die. (EC, p. 177)

This ever-changing façade of the empirical world is visualized as the tossing sea in "The Dry Salvages" and depicted in all its immeasurable flux of terror and despair. The central metaphor of the second section of "The Dry Salvages" is that of men adrift at sea, desperately toiling to keep chaos at bay and to find a momentary stay against confusion in the ceaseless flux:

> Where is the end of them, the fishermen sailing
> Into the wind's tail, where the fog cowers?
> . . . .
> We have to think of them as forever bailing,
> Setting and hauling, while the North East lowers
> Over shallow banks unchanging and erosionless
> Or drawing their money, drying sails at dockage;
> Not as making a trip that will be unpayable
> For a haul that will not bear examination. (DS, p. 196)

Change, then, is constant; it is manifested in endless cycles of birth, growth, decay, and death in the objective world of phenomena; it is also extended to the subjective world of impressions in the third section of "The Dry Salvages," so that no individuality or ego can be preserved from the flux:

> Fare forward, travellers! not escaping from the past
> Into different lives, or into any future;
> You are not the same people who left that station

> Or who will arrive at any terminus,
> While the narrowing rails slide together behind you;
>
> . . . .
>
> "Fare forward, you who think that you are voyaging;
> You are not those who saw the harbour
> Receding, or those who will disembark." (DS, pp. 187-88)

The frightening underworld of the London subway has already been evoked in "Burnt Norton," where men and women are in limbo, neither dead nor alive, whirled about by circumstance like bits of paper in the wind. They are, in fact, inhabitants of death's twilight kingdom, latter-day incarnations of the hollow men, whose souls have shriveled up and reveal only straw or emptiness:

> Here is a place of disaffection
> Time before and time after
> In a dim light: neither daylight
> Investing form with lucid stillness
> Turning shadow into transient beauty
> With slow rotation suggesting permanence
> Nor darkness to purify the soul
> . . . Only a flicker
> Over the strained time-ridden faces
> Distracted from distraction by distraction
> Filled with fancies and empty of meaning
> Tumid apathy with no concentration
> Men and bits of paper, whirled by the cold wind
> That blows before and after time. (BN, pp. 173-74)

The overtones of irony and pathos reinforce the basic existential fact of impermanence.

The description of universal suffering is even more graphic than that of flux in Eliot's poetry. Perhaps nowhere else is the pervasiveness of suffering more poignantly evoked than in the second section of "The Dry Salvages":

> Where is there an end of it, the soundless wailing,
> The silent withering of autumn flowers
> Dropping their petals and remaining motionless;
> Where is there an end to the drifting wreckage,
> The prayer of the bone on the beach, the unprayable
> Prayer at the calamitous annunciation?
>
> . . . .

There is no end of it, the voiceless wailing,
No end to the withering of withered flowers,
To the movement of pain that is painless and motionless,
To the drift of the sea and the drifting wreckage,
The bone's prayer to Death its God. (DS, p. 186)

This apprehension of existence in the empirical world is not the outcome of logical analysis. It is rather a tragic vision of life, grasped in all its immediacy of horror and despair, as Kurtz glimpses it in his dying moment, or as Tiresias sees it in his remembrance of things past. It is even doubtful whether the impermanence and suffering are ever fully grasped, for mankind cannot bear too much reality.

2

THE WHEEL

This vast universe is a wheel. Upon it are all creatures that are subject to birth, death and rebirth. Round and round it turns and never stops. It is the wheel of Brahman. As long as the individual self thinks it is separate from Brahman, it revolves upon the wheel in bondage to the laws of birth, death and rebirth. But when through the grace of Brahman it realizes its identity with him, it revolves upon the wheel no longer. It achieves immortality.

SVETASVATARA UPANISHAD

The human predicament in the midst of omnipresent and universal change and suffering is often expressed in Vedanta and Buddhism by the image of the wheel. Krishna speaks of the terrible wheel of birth and death which binds the individual down to the phenomenal world of time and circumstance: "The spirit of man when in nature feels the ever-changing conditions of nature. When he binds himself to things ever-changing, a good or evil fate whirls him round through life-in-death."[1] And the Buddha alludes to the wheel of existence, which he calls *saṁsāra*:

The Wheel of Existence is without known beginning ...
The Wheel of Existence is empty with a twelvefold emptiness.
Respecting the Wheel of Existence it is to be understood that
   the two factors ignorance and desire are its roots.
Ignorance, desire and attachment form the round of the
   corruptions ...
And it is through these three that this Wheel of Existence is
   said to have three rounds ... it is incessant ... it revolves.[2]

The symbolism of the wheel is not alien to Christian thought either. In fact, as the Plotinian scholar, W.R. Inge,—with whose writings Eliot was probably familiar—points out, the early Christian era was permeated with the realization that the chief aim of mankind should be "to escape from the 'weary wheel' of earthly existence and to find rest in the bosom of the eternal."[3] The image of the wheel is in the New Testament: the phrase in James 3:6, "setteth on fire the course of nature," is a free translation of the Greek word meaning wheel. The Oxford annotated edition of the Bible explicates it as "the wheel of birth."[4]

Many expounders of Plato's doctrine of time have found the wheel or the circle an appropriate symbol of the relation between time and eternity, so that the circumference of the wheel may be said to represent the world of created things in time and the centre of the wheel the timeless realm of God.[5] The image of the wheel also serves as the best illustration of Plotinus' picture of the universe. The relation between the three parts of his Trinity— the One, the Spirit, and the Soul—can be described as the relation between two concentric circles and their common centre, the centre representing the One, the inner circle the Spirit, and the outer circle the Soul. In the final analysis, the symbol of the wheel may be said to split up the world order into two essentially different factors: rotary movement and immobility—or the circumference of the wheel and its still centre, an image of the Aristotelean "unmoved mover." This becomes a dominant theme in mystical philosophy and persists into the Middle Ages, so that even the ornamental oculi of Romanesque churches and rose windows of Gothic cathedrals are patterned on the wheel. During the Renaissance, the wheel is absorbed into a popular adage—God is a Circle, whose circumference is nowhere and whose centre is everywhere.[6]

The image of the wheel also occurs in Shakespeare's *King Lear*. Towards the end, Lear, a greatly saddened and much wiser man, declares to Cordelia: "Thou art a soul in bliss, but I am bound/ Upon a wheel of fire."[7] Similar metaphors, probably derived from Neo-Platonic sources, abound in metaphysical poetry. Donne, for instance, uses the image of the circle and the unmoving centre in "The Second Anniversarie":

> Then, Soule, to thy first pitch worke up againe;
> Know that all lines which circles doe containe,
> For once that they the Center touch, doe touch
> Twice the circumference; and be thou such;
> Double on heaven thy thoughts on earth emploid;
> All will not serve; only who have enjoy'd
> The sight of God, in fulnesse, can thinke it;
> For it is both the object, and the wit.[8]

The wheel may even be regarded as an archetypal symbol expressing a fundamental fact of human existence, as T.E. Hulme observes in his *Speculations:*

> It is the closing of all roads, this realisation of the tragic significance of life, which makes it legitimate to call all other attitudes shallow. Such a realisation has formed the basis of all great religions, and is most conveniently remembered by the symbol of the wheel. This symbol of the futility of existence is absolutely lost to the modern world, nor can it be recovered without great difficulty.[9]

It may, however, be poignantly evoked in poetry by a sensitive and discriminating use of language.

The symbolism of the wheel is not explicitly present in Eliot's poems published before *The Waste Land*. However, it is implicit in the tone and manner of certain vivid passages. Prufrock's existence, for instance, is enveloped, literally and metaphorically, in an ever-swirling fog:

> The yellow fog that rubs its back upon the window-panes
> The yellow smoke that rubs its muzzle on the window-panes,
> Licked its tongue into the corners of the evening,
> Lingered upon the pools that stand in drains . . .
> *Curled* once about the house, and fell asleep. (LP, p. 13; my emphasis)

The sameness Prufrock encounters everywhere in his harsh urban existence produces in him an extreme weariness of spirit; his life seems to revolve around the taking of toast and tea, and the meeting of women who "come and go/ Talking of Michelangelo" (LP, p. 14).

The speaker in "Preludes" is almost an extension of the Prufrockian personality. He is obsessed by the desolation of the urban landscape, and the sordid lives of its inhabitants convulse him with pity, so that he yearns for a redeeming compassionate figure:

> I am moved by fancies that are *curled*
> Around these images, and cling;
> The notion of some infinitely gentle
> Infinitely suffering thing. (P, p. 23; my emphasis)

A Buddha or a Christ, however, is nowhere in evidence, and so he takes refuge in cynicism: "Wipe your hand across your mouth, and laugh;/ The worlds *revolve* like ancient women/ Gathering fuel in vacant lots" (P, p. 23; my emphasis). It is the defiant gesture of a person who is compelled to bear witness to a spectacle of suffering unrelieved by any hope of redemption, of one who is appalled by the cyclic purposelessness of day-to-day existence vividly represented by the futile circling of ancient women in vacant lots. Despite the mocking tone of the speaker, his pained awareness of suffering as an inescapable fact of existence comes through, and the recurrent pattern of suffering and despair is represented by a striking archetypal image, an image strongly suggestive of a revolving wheel.

Gerontion is an old man with "thoughts of a dry brain in a dry season" (G, p. 39). Yet he is acutely conscious of the vacuity of his existence and suffers intensely because of it. The flurry of foreign names he recalls from his former life—Mr. Silvero, Hakagawa, Madame de Tornquist, Fraülein von Kulp, De Bailhache, Fresca, Mrs. Cammel—evokes a cosmopolitan world of finance and corruption. But all these people are merely part of a gyrating, whirling humanity, ultimately producing only emptiness. In the final analysis, they have no reality, "whirled/ Beyond the circuit of the shuddering Bear/ In fractured atoms" (G, p. 39). They are no more important than a dead gull in the windy straits of Belle Isle or Cape Horn or an old man driven by the trade winds to a sleepy corner. Their fate epitomizes the general disintegration of life and suggests the universal human predicament. Though Gerontion never actually uses the image of the wheel, his yearning to escape from "the weary wheel of earthly existence" and to find "rest in the bosom of the eternal"[10] certainly comes through his meditations.

Apparently, by the time he came to write *The Waste Land*, Eliot had thoroughly digested the Hindu-Buddhist ideas he became acquainted with at Harvard and assimilated them in his poetry. According to Herbert Howarth, he

> preached the Buddhist askesis in *The Waste Land*. He preached a new askesis, the Buddhist renunciation in Christian guise, in his essays on education in the late twenties and thirties, urged it by the example of Becket and the example of Agatha and Harry, urged in "Little Gidding" the cultivation of "detachment of self from things and persons," and in *The Cocktail Party* again described the saint's renunciation of the world.[11]

We know, moreover, that he seriously contemplated becoming a Buddhist when he wrote *The Waste Land* and that he incorporated the Buddha's Fire Sermon as well as the *Brihad-aranyaka Upanishad* in the poem.

Not surprisingly, therefore, the image of the wheel figures prominently in *The Waste Land*. For instance, the cyclical process of birth, copulation, and death is reinforced in the opening section by Madame Sosostris, who describes people literally going round in circles: "I see crowds of people, walking

University of Winnipeg, 515 Portage Ave., Winnipeg, Manitoba, Canada R3B 2E9

round in a ring" (*WL*, p. 62). Significantly, in the first and final drafts of "The Burial of the Dead," Madame Sosostris picks out a Tarot card containing the image of "The Wheel" (note Eliot's capitalization of the word) (*WL*, p. 62). It is clear that Eliot is evoking the image of the wheel, explicitly as well as implicitly, in order to convey the hopeless predicament of "the crowds of people" doomed to repeat their lives endlessly:

> A crowd flowed over London Bridge, so many,
> I had not thought death had undone so many.
> Sighs, short and infrequent, were exhaled,
> And each man fixed his eyes before his feet.
> Flowed up the hill and down King William street,
> To where Saint Mary Woolnoth kept the hours
> With a dead sound on the final stroke of nine. (*WL*, p. 62)

It is a meaningless existence, bound forever by space, time, and circumstance, like that of the Cumaean Sibyl, and the horror stems from the fact that most of these people are not even fully conscious of the utter vacuity of their lives.

The description of the lives of the London crowds is again touched upon in the first draft of "The Fire Sermon":

> London, the swarming life you kill and breed,
> Huddled between the concrete and the sky,
> Responsive to the momentary need,
> Vibrates unconscious to its formal destiny.[12]

These lines are crossed out in the manuscript by Ezra Pound, who edited the poem, and the margin carries his terse comment: B____ s.[11] Justified, perhaps, from an aesthetic point of view, for poetry loses its intensity from too much elaboration. The last line, however, is singled out by Eliot, who makes a faint pencil mark—"Keep"—beside it in the margin, but he omits the line in his final draft. Nor does he retain the crucial line which follows and explains what the "formal destiny" of London's "swarming life" is: "London, your people is bound upon the wheel."[13] This assertion is repeated two lines later and reappears in a slightly modified form elsewhere in the manuscript: "The inhabitants of Hampstead are bound forever on the wheel."[14] Following Pound's advice and guided by his own instinct, Eliot does not include these lines in his final version, but it is clear that he draws heavily on the symbolism of the wheel in his pathetic evocation of the death-in-life of the London crowds.

Is Eliot thinking of the medieval wheel of fate when he includes the wheel in Madame Sosostris' pack of cards? Philip Wheelwright has, in fact, identified the wheel of "Burnt Norton" as the Wheel of Fortune,[15] a common meaning of the wheel in Shakespeare and other Renaissance authors. Such an identification is possible in the case of *The Waste Land* too, but the identification pays too much attention to the popular, iconographic aspects of the symbol, neglecting its primary philosophical meaning, one closely related to ancient Greek and Indian theories of time. Philosophically speaking, the wheel of birth and death (*saṁsāra*) in Hindu-Buddhist thought is more universal and includes the symbolism of the medieval wheel of fate, which represents the fluctuations in the fortunes of an individual, the fall from a high to a low state, and the rise from a low to a high state. It is possible, according to the Hindu-Buddhist notion of metempsychosis, to be incarnated in a lower as well as higher order of existence.[16] There is a rather striking example of this 'fall' from a higher to a lower incarnation in the change of Philomela into a nightingale, which Eliot adapts from Ovid's *Metamorphoses*:

The change of Philomel, by the barbarous king
So rudely forced; yet there the nightingale
Filled all the desert with inviolable voice
And still she *cried*, and still the world *pursues*. (*WL*, p.64; my emphasis)

The abrupt change from the past to the present tense in the last line indicates that this is an ongoing process: loss of innocence and purity entails reincarnation in a lower order of existence, which may be symbolically represented by a lower curve of the revolving wheel.

In fact, this continuous process of metempsychosis and the associated symbolism of the wheel are frequently illustrated in "A Game of Chess."[17] There is, at first, the decline of royalty: Cleopatra, Queen of Egypt, magnificently described through blank verse in the opening lines, fades into the anonymous typist, awaiting the carbuncular young man in her room. (The 'fall' is reflected even in the deterioration of the blank verse into jiggling rhymes.) The splendour of the Egyptian Queen is subtly undermined by the inconsequential chatter of her modern prototype—"O O O O that Shakespeherian Rag" (*WL*, p. 65) and "the burnished throne" of the former yields place to "a closed car at four" (*WL*, pp. 64-65). Vitality and purposefulness, in other words, have been sapped, leaving apathy and aimlessness to reign in their place.

The series of "Goonights" (*WL*, p. 66) at the end of "A Game of Chess" is a poignant yet vulgarized echo of another Danish girl, Ophelia, who was ill-treated by a prince. The echo preserves the Shakespearian backdrop of the entire scenario in "A Game of Chess"; at the same time, it is Shakespeare reincarnated and modernized, at the lower turn of the wheel.

Further evidence of Eliot's use of metempsychosis and the symbolism of the wheel comes from the manuscript of *The Waste Land*. Even before he chooses Ovid's Philomela, he toys with the idea of lower incarnations in a general and unspecified manner. Thus, he hints darkly at the probable future condition of the inhabitants of Hampstead:

> Dog's eyes reaching over the table
> Are in their heads when they stare
> Supposing that they have the heads of birds
> Beaks and no words . . .
> I should like to be in a crowd of beaks without words.[18]

It is illuminating to compare the idea expressed here obliquely with the Lama's exposition of metempsychosis in *Kim*:

> When the shadows shortened and the Lama leaned more heavily upon Kim, there was always the Wheel of Life to draw forth . . . Here sat the Gods on high—and they were the dreams of dreams. Here was our Heaven and the world of the demi-Gods—horsemen fighting among the hills. Here were the agonies done upon beasts, souls ascending or descending the ladder . . . Often the Lama made living pictures the matter of his text, bidding Kim . . . note how the flesh takes a thousand thousand shapes, desirable or detestable as men reckon, but in truth of no account either way; and how the stupid spirit is bound to follow the body through all the Heavens and all the Hells, and strictly round again.[19]

This is, in fact, the main thrust of *The Waste Land*. The blind Tiresias *sees* all the different lives of his past unroll before him; he bears witness to the flesh "taking a thousand thousand shapes" in lower as well as higher incarnations.[20] He is not impersonating them; he *contains* them all in his comprehensive gnostic vision; he *is* all these different beings: "And I Tiresias have foresuffered all/ Enacted on the same divan or bed" (*WL*, p. 69). The human incarnations range over a wide social spectrum, including queens as well as washerwomen, heroes and saints of yore as well as charlatans and sinners of today—they are all manifestations of the flesh "taking a thousand thousand shapes," according to the law of *karma* (the volitional acts of an individual which determine the nature of his subsequent lives). It is theoretically possible, therefore, for the poem to include many more lives than those already present. Bleistein and Fresca, for instance, could well have figured in the final version of the poem. Bleistein's avarice rules his actions and these constitute his *karma*, determining the nature of his succeeding existence. Consequently, his next life will resemble his present one: "Though he suffers a sea change/ Still expensive and strange."[21] As for Fresca, her present life is the fruit of her past *karma*; the circumstances surrounding her life have changed but her nature remains essentially the same. Hence, Fresca "in another time and place had been . . ./ The lazy laughing Jenny of the Bard."[22] The faces may be different, but the *karma* does not change; and so the wheel turns a full circle, throwing up similar lives again and again:

> (The same eternal and consuming itch
> Can make a martyr, or plain simple bitch);
> . . . .
> For varying forms, one definition's right:
> Unreal emotions, and real appetite.[23]

Why did Pound strike off the lines describing these characters, reinforcing the theme of reincarnation or metempsychosis? His objections were probably aesthetic. Obviously, the poem would have suffered from the inclusion of too many examples illustrating the same concept. Moreover, a little ambiguity adds richness and intensity. This is equally true of the long sea voyage Pound deleted, since it essentially conveys the same idea of reincarnation. The voyage represents in a modern guise the journey of Ulysses in Canto XXVI of the *Inferno* and includes an anachronistic encounter with the sirens:

> On watch, I thought I saw in the fore cross-trees
> Three women leaning forward, with white hair
> Streaming behind, who sang above the wind
> A song that charmed my senses.[24]

The speaker fancies that it is a dream, but actually it is his memory of a former life.

Incidentally, this explains why Stetson is hailed as a former acquaintance in the opening section—"You who were with me in the ships at Mylae!" (*WL*, p. 62). The speaker means exactly what he says: Stetson too is a reincarnation; he has been associated with Tiresias in a former birth. The quick recognition indicates that Tiresias has grown in self-awareness through his innumerable lives, while his ready acceptance of the former life and its association suggests the maturing of his wisdom.

Similarly, the dog at the end of the opening section is the Websterian wolf reincarnated, but with a curious change in character. The wolf in *The White Devil* was a "foe" to be feared, but the dog in *The Waste Land* is a "friend to men" (*WL*, p. 63). It digs up the buried corpse of the corn god of the vegetation myths and prevents the corpse from sprouting and flowering, thereby ending resurrection. In other words, reincarnation, not death, is to be feared and avoided, since it binds one forever to the wheel. Tiresias' earlier offer to show "fear in a handful of dust" (*WL*, p. 61) refers not to death but to the dubious immortality of the Sibyl who was granted "a life of as many years as she had grains of dust in her hand."[25]

Thus, when "you come to the brass tacks" (*FA*, p. 122) like Sweeney, existence is a nightmare, an endless cycle of birth, copulation, and death. To be helplessly bound to the time-conditioned wheel of *saṁsāra*, to be blindly caught up in its revolutions without realizing its evanescence, is *avidyā* or ignorance; not to seek a way out of this endless cycle is to be involved in perpetual suffering. Hence, an air of unreality pervades the lives of the inhabitants of London or Hampstead, and because the turns of the wheel are universally applicable, what is true of London is also true of other cities:

> Falling towers
> Jerusalem Athens Alexandria
> Vienna London
> Unreal (*WL*, p. 73)

The Jewish, Greek and Egyptian civilizations have all declined and disappeared; modern civilizations will follow them. Those who inhabit the cities, the centres of modern civilization, are all ghosts of former lives, essentially re-enacting the same roles. The wheel keeps turning:

> . . . The nymphs are departed.
> Sweet Thames, run softly, till I end my song.
>   . . . The nymphs are departed.
> And their friends, the loitering heirs of City directors;
> Departed, have left no addresses . . .
> But at my back in a cold blast I hear
> The rattle of bones, and chuckle spread from ear to ear. (*WL*, p. 67)

The bones are *alive*; their chuckling underscores the horror, not of death, as the allusion to Marvell might lead us to expect, but of rebirth and endless suffering. Reincarnation, not death, is to be dreaded.

Death brings no relief, then, being but a prelude to another life; in fact, the moment of death causes intense agony, for, like Kurtz or Phlebas the Phoenecian, Everyman has to live his life all over again, without any real hope of a magical sea-change into something rich and strange:

> A current under sea
> Picked his bones in whispers. As he rose and fell
> He passed the stages of his age and youth
> Entering the *whirlpool*. (*WL*, p. 71; my emphasis)

The inexorable revolutions of the wheel claim Everyman at death and lead to his rebirth. The point is made even more clearly in the French account of Phlebas the Phoenecian in "Dans le Restaurant": "Le repassant aux étapes de sa vie antérieure" (DR, p.51). Eliot is here recalling Baudelaire's "La vie antérieure," of which Wallace Stevens writes: "The idea of an earlier life is like the idea of a later life, or like the idea of a different life, part of the classic repertory of poetic subjects."[26] Eliot uses this "classic repertory" with such controlled skill that it no longer belongs to the realm of the ordinary.

An intriguing example of his use of this repertory is found in the invitation to "Come in under the shadow of this red rock" (*WL*, p. 61) in the opening section of *The Waste Land*. The passage first occurs in a fragment called "The Death of St. Narcissus." It begins as a description of a narcissistic man struck mad "by the knowledge of his own beauty," but, in a later version, becomes an exposition of metempsychosis. Consider, for instance, the following lines: "First he *wished* that he had been a tree/ To push its branches among each other" (my emphasis).[27] The stress here is on egotistic self-indulgence in fantasy. The emphasis shifts in the later version to the remembrance of a former mode of existence: "First he was *sure* that he had been a tree" (my emphasis).[28] Similarly, the lines "Then he *wished* that he had been a fish/ With slippery white belly held between his own fingers/ To have writhed in his own clutch" (my emphasis)[29] are modified into "Then he *knew* that he had been a fish" (my emphasis).[30] Last but not the least, the man's desire to change his sex and be raped—"Then he *wished* he had been a young girl/ Caught in the woods by a drunken old man/ To have known at the last moment, the full taste of her own whiteness" (my emphasis)[31]—is accomplished in the final version: "Then he *had been* a young girl" (my emphasis).[32] Why does Eliot deliberately make these changes? Probably because he wants to describe a series of previous incarnations or "vies antérieures" and reinforce the theme of reincarnation.

It is also interesting that the higher form of existence supersedes the lower in this series. Out of insentient matter—the tangled roots and branches—is forged a living tree; the tree gives place to the fish, a mobile creature endowed with instincts, and the fish gives place to a girl, a thinking and feeling human being. It is evolution in miniature, from matter to vegetable, from vegetable to animal, from animal to man. What is the next link in this Great Chain of Being? God, surely. This is the answer Eliot posits in his later poetry, though he uses an impersonal philosophical language to indicate this ultimate link in the chain. He calls it the still point of the turning world—the centre, so to speak, of the revolving wheel.[33]

Taken in isolation, however, without the counterbalancing notion of the still centre, the symbolism of the wheel and its associated concepts of change and suffering constitute a vision of despair, a vision presented with such skill that even the most enterprising reader of this poetry might draw back in dismay, overwhelmed by its unrelieved bleakness. Given the fundamental perception of *universal* change and suffering, there *seems* to be no escape from the terrible wheel of birth and death; it stops not for the widow's tear or the orphan's cry, but grinds on, crushing everything in its path. Fortunately, this profound despair is offset by an equally profound hope of freedom from bondage to the wheel and of peace that passes understanding. Even in the Waste Land, there is the *promise* of rain.

In the final section, "What the Thunder Said," the symbolism of the wheel and its associated concept of metempsychosis are blended with the Christian idea of resurrection and eternal life as well as the vegetation myth of the corn god who dies yearly and is resurrected. Thus, the section begins with an allusion to the arrest, suffering and death of Christ:

> After the torchlight red on sweaty faces
> After the frosty silence in the gardens
> After the agony in stony places
> The shouting and the crying
> Prison and place and reverberation. (*WL*, p. 72)

Then comes a description of the "thunder of spring over distant mountains" with its promise of rain that will resurrect the buried god and make the crops grow. The section concludes with a collection of fragments that, as we shall see later, reinforce the theme of reincarnation and suggest the possibility of release from the endless cycle of birth and death.

Eliot's treatment of Christian resurrection is rather unorthodox and even pessimistic. The Gospels clearly identify the figure that accompanies the apostles on the road to Emmaus—it is the risen Christ, triumphant over death and promising eternal life. The figure in Eliot's poem is more ambiguous and provokes doubtful enquiries:

> Who is the third who always walks beside you
> When I count, there are only you and I together
> But when I look ahead up the white road
> There is always another one walking beside you
> Gliding wrapt in a brown mantle, hooded
> I do not know whether a man or a woman
> —But who is that on the other side of you? (*WL*, p. 73)

It is not even certain whether the figure is a man or a woman. Moreover, Eliot himself suggests in his notes that the apparition is a simple hallucination. He says that the lines were stimulated by an Antarctic expedition in which "the party of explorers ... had the *constant delusion* that there was *one more member* than could actually be counted" (*WL*, p. 79). Apparently, Eliot subjects the risen Christ to the Hindu-Buddhist ideas of reincarnation and the illusory nature (*māyā*) of existence. Is Eliot playing the doubting Thomas? This seems to be the case, especially when we consider the account of the Chapel Perilous a few lines later: the Chapel is empty, except for a crowing cock—a reminder of Peter's doubt and denial.

Lacking the assurance of a saviour, Tiresias remains bound to the wheel and his soul is imprisoned in the flesh yet again:

>   I have heard the key
> Turn in the door once and turn once only
> We think of the key, each in his prison
> Thinking of the key, each confirms a prison (*WL*, p. 74)

But his situation is not entirely hopeless. He does have some knowledge of the nature of existence and some awareness of the agony resulting from the recurring cycle of births and deaths. So he is able to sympathize (*dayadhvam*) with his fellow-beings and to control (*damyata*) his own destiny to some extent: "Only at nightfall, aetherial rumors/ Revive for a moment a broken Coriolanus" (*WL*, p. 74). Cities and their inhabitants may fall again and again in the inevitable cycle, but at least the narrator has grown enough in self-awareness to "set his lands in order" (*WL*, p. 74).

The cyclic quality of birth and death merges easily with the vegetation myth of the corn god who is repeatedly buried and revived. All life constantly renews itself as the wheel keeps turning; hence, the poem encompasses a full year's cycle, from spring to winter, in the opening section. Moreover, the symbolism of the wheel explains the complex image of joyless spring at the beginning of the poem. April is "the cruellest month" (*WL*, p. 61) precisely because it mixes the "memory" of former existences in vanished cities with the "desire" for evanescent things of the world and causes the wheel to revolve, entangling mankind in the web of *māyā* and reincarnation: or, as the *Gita* puts it, "Their soul is warped with selfish desires, and their heaven in a selfish desire. They have prayers for pleasures and power, the reward of which is earthly rebirth."[34] Spring only renews old agonies. This is why, in "The Fire Sermon," the narrator dwells on the horror, not of death, but of seasonal regeneration through the union of Sweeney and Mrs. Porter in the spring (*WL*, p. 67).

Towards the end, Tiresias, seeker of reality who contains the Fisher King and the questing knight within himself, sets his "lands in order" and shores up certain "fragments" against the ruins of former lives (*WL*, pp. 74-75). These fragments reinforce the idea of reincarnation: the first translates into "Then he dived back into the fire that refines them" (*WL*, p. 75) and conveys the notion of purification through purgation—an exact parallel to the idea of evolution toward *nirvāṇa* through metempsychosis (the individual soul refines itself through successive lives till it attains freedom); the second recalls the reincarnation of Philomela as a nightingale, an archetypal process in the universe, whenever innocence is violated; the third equates the disinheritance and consequent sense of loss in a former life to Tiresias' present yearning to be free and at peace; the fourth alludes to Hieronymo, who feigns madness and stages a play, in which the actors speak "in unknown languages" and enact different roles that reflect their real lives, but which is intended to prove "the invention and all was good"[35]—the wheel of birth and death involves us in many different lives and causes pain and suffering, but impels us in the end to seek and attain *nirvāṇa*. The poem concludes by reiterating the instructions received from the thunder—Give, Sympathize, and Control— and intoning the formal invocation of the Upanishads—Shanti Shanti Shanti—a fitting reminder that ultimately the peace that passes understanding will prevail; the revolutions of the wheel will eventually be annulled by its central peace—the turning world will be overcome by the still point.

Unlike *The Waste Land, The Hollow Men* does not have multiple levels of meaning. *The Waste Land* projects universal change and suffering through a montage of individual lives bound on the wheel, so that the cumulative impression is of mankind oblivious to reality, to the still point of the turning world. We are confronted, in other words, with a terrifying "heap of broken images," terrifying not merely because they are broken, but because they are so numerous. Precisely the same spiritual *Angst* is implied in *The Hollow Men*, though it is not so richly illustrated; consequently, the poem is a lyrical and symbolic comment on the spiritual distress occasioned by bondage to the turning wheel. The predicament of the hollow men is the same as that of the wastelanders; they lack the "courage to be" and have lost their reality because they have never affirmed it. Their *malaise* is not that they have evil impulses, but that they have no impulses at all. They are so full of inertia that they are remembered "not as lost/ Violent souls, but only/ As the hollow men/ The stuffed men" (*HM*, p. 83). Their lives are empty, not because life as a whole is meaningless and futile but because they evade responsibility for their acts and refuse to acknowledge that life has a purpose beyond survival and reproduction. Their bondage to the cycle of birth and death is vividly captured in their dance around the prickly pear. The sing-song effect of their chant ironically underscores the pathos and emptiness of their lives. They decline to assert their freedom by spiritual and moral choice; instead, they act arbitrarily, gratifying their most immediate needs, quite unmindful of any transcending ideal. In short, they are blindly caught up in the revolutions of the wheel.

But there *are* a few sensitive souls who are not enslaved by the turns of the wheel and consciously turn towards the still point. *Ash Wednesday* records the penitential experience of such a soul. The theme of turning is frequently repeated in the poem and seems related to the beginning of the epistle on Ash Wednesday: "Therefore also now, saith the Lord, turn ye even unto me with all your heart, and with fasting, and with weeping, and with mourning: And rend your heart, and not your garments, and turn unto the Lord your God."[36] There is a sermon on this text by Lancelot Andrewes which begins with an allusion to the image of the turning wheel:

> Now at this time is the turning of the year . . . . Everything now turning that we also would make it our time to turn to God in . . . Upon this turning, *cardo vertitur*, the hinge turns, of our well and evil doing for ever . . . Repentance itself is nothing but a kind of circling . . . Which circle consists of two turnings . . . . First a turn wherein we look forward to God and with our whole heart resolve to turn to Him. Then a turn again wherein we look backward to our sins wherein we have turned from God . . . . The wheel turns apace, and if we turn not the rather these turnings may overtake us.[37]

It is well-known that Eliot admired Andrewes, wrote a long essay on him, and incorporated his sayings in his poetry and drama. He was probably influenced, therefore, by this sermon in his exploration of the implications of the turning wheel in *Ash Wednesday*. This does not mean, however, that Eliot has discarded the Hindu-Buddhist concept of the wheel, for he does evoke the perceptions of impermanence and suffering in the poem. It only means that he is blending Christian and Hindu-Buddhist concepts, an experiment he attempts on a deeper level in *Four Quartets*.

Ash Wednesday, as a whole, suggests a change of direction in the life of the speaker, away from the turning world towards the still point. It also conveys something of the inconstancy of the human will, which is apt to turn back to the temptations from which it has turned away. Consequently, a sense of insecurity as well as an awareness of the conscious effort required in turning towards the still point pervade the poem. They indicate that the faith towards which the poem strives should not induce complacency and that submission to the divine will does not mean inertia.

The protagonist has not attained spiritual enlightenment by the end of the poem; he has merely had tantalizing glimpses of the peace that comes through the surrender of the self to the divine will. Hence, he prays for detachment from the evanescent things of this world and for compassion towards all suffering beings: "Teach us to care and not to care/ Teach us to sit still" (*AW*, p. 98). He now perceives that his struggle to turn away from the temptations of the world towards the reality of the still point is part of the travail of creation; it is a universal human predicament to be torn between the whirligig of the world and the peace of eternity. He can also sense that the movement of the world seems contrary to the stillness of the divine Word that is this peace. Hence, the world does not recognize the Word when it appears in the guise of a Krishna, a Buddha, or a Christ; instead, the world rebels against the Word and even crucifies it when it is incarnate in the flesh: "Against the Word the unstilled world still whirled/ About the centre of the silent Word" (*AW*, p. 96). By rejecting the Word, the world enchains itself ever more firmly to the wheel and experiences continual change and suffering. Yet, paradoxically, the Word is central to all existence and activity in the world. This concept of the world revolving around the Word is precisely evoked by the image of the wheel turning about its still centre.

The vision of the human condition projected in *Four Quartets* is less perlexed, though no less complex, than that in *The Waste Land*. Both poems stress the universality of change and suffering and communicate the spiritual torment that ensues from bondage to the wheel, but what is only the faintest spark of hope in *The Waste Land*, "a damp gust bringing rain" (*WL*, p. 74), becomes a positive blaze of faith in *Four Quartets*. Even the conflict between the temporal and eternal values, so prominent in *Ash Wednesday*, has lost its intensity owing to a sharper apprehension of that greater pattern in which all contraries are transcended. Within this pattern, all the discordant symptoms of the *malaise* of the wastelanders—the quest for certainty and freedom, the need to love and be loved, the longing for grace—assume a heightened significance; they are all now seen as temporal manifestations of the eternal confrontation between man and God.

In order to portray the confrontation in all its complexity, Eliot reverts to the symbolism of the wheel. He never actually uses the term 'wheel' as he does in the manuscripts of *The Waste Land*. Instead, he evokes it by a skilful use of words and situations so that the image is completed in our minds.

The movement of the world against the Word has already been described strikingly and unforgettably in *Ash Wednesday*. The second section of "Burnt Norton" begins by alluding to the temptations of the turning world which cloud human perception and hinder the apprehension of the still centre: "Garlic and sapphires in the mud/ Clot the bedded axle-tree" (*BN*, p. 172). According to Grover Smith, garlic and sapphires stand for gluttony and avarice, while mud suggests filth and the weakness of the flesh.[38] These imperfections prevent the wheel from turning freely. The "bedded axle-tree" corresponds to the image of 'the still centre' introduced a few lines later and represents the point of contact between man and God, around which all activities, human and non-human, revolve. When this central axle is clogged by the impurities of the flesh, the movement of the wheel, man's active life in the world, is impeded and appears to be meaningless and futile. Nevertheless, it is still possible for man to overcome his limitations and apprehend a divine order in which the impediment is nullified, a greater pattern in which the apparently contradictory forces of his being are reconciled. In other words, it is still possible for man to intuit "the still point of the turning world" (BN, p. 173). This cryptic yet precise description vividly brings to mind the image of the wheel turning about is central axis. The image has multiple connotations: it highlights the apparent opposition between the unmoved Mover and the cyclical activity of His creation, between eternity and time, and illustrates the intimate relationship between God and the world, the eternal and the temporal.

When man overcomes the limitations of the flesh and gains even a momentary apprehension of the still centre, he has an intuitive revelation of

>   both a new world
> And the old made explicit, understood
> In the completion of its partial ecstasy
> The resolution of its partial horror. (BN, p. 173)

The moment of ecstasy does not belie the agony that comes before and after; it merely invests man with a fresh insight into the change and suffering that pervade the world. The apprehension of the still point enables him to understand the merry-go-round of temporal life in the light of eternity; he learns to live in harmony with the noumenal reality so that the flux and suffering of the phenomenal world no longer cause him spiritual anguish. The wheel turns smoothly about its central axle, its movement no longer checked by human imperfections. Such a harmonious life is charmingly depicted in "East Coker" through the dignified dancing of the country people around a bonfire:

> Round and round the bonfire
> Leaping through the flames, or joined in circles,
> Rustically solemn or in rustic laughter
> Lifting heavy feet in clumsy shoes
> Earth feet, loam feet, lifted in country mirth
> Mirth of those long since under earth
> Nourishing the corn. (EC, p. 178)

It is a scene of wholesome rustic simplicity, very different from the dismaying spectacle of the Wastelanders going round and round in circles or of the Hollow Men enacting a horrible caricature of a dance round and round the prickly pear. Not only does this "daunsinge" signify "matrimonie," it also tells of the concord of men and women who, ordering their lives in obedience to the natural rhythms, "The time of the seasons and the constellations/ The time of milking and the time of harvest" (EC, p. 178), are in harmony with the universe. Their lives are even intimately associated with those of the "beasts": "The time of the coupling of man and woman/ And that of beasts. Feet rising and falling,/ Eating and drinking. Dung and death" (EC, p. 178). A summing up, far removed in tone from Sweeney's cynical assessment of life in "Fragment of an Agon": "That's all the facts when you come to the brass tacks: Birth, and copulation, and death" (FA, p. 122). The cycle of birth, reproduction, and death remains the same for the men and women dancing round the bonfire, but it assumes a greater significance, because it contributes to a harmonious whole.

Nowhere does Eliot completely elucidate the concept of the wheel and its relation to the still point, but by piecing together his overt and covert allusions to the wheel we may understand its significance. The wheel keeps turning, symbolizing the ceaseless flux of existence. The various forms of life in the world, vegetable, animal, and human, are whirled about by the wheel, finding themselves at a higher or lower curve of the wheel, according to their individual *karma*, in their successive lives; consequently, they are all bound to the wheel and are subject to endless suffering. It is possible, however, for a sensitive human being to be free of this bondage and to live harmoniously by apprehending the still centre of the wheel and understanding the turning world in terms of the still point, so that the apparent contradictions between them are resolved in the light of eternity. The moment of apprehension comes not by human will but by divine grace; yet one has to be ready for it, repenting of past errors and preparing oneself through "prayer, observance, discipline, thought and action" (DS, p. 190).

This is the kind of preparation Thomas Becket undertakes in *Murder in the Cathedral*. Becket is the contemplative *par excellence*; that he has meditated long and deep over man's responsibilities to God and his fellow beings is evident in all his words and deeds. He knows that change and suffering are inseparable from existence and that the phenomenal world seems opposed to the reality of the noumenon. But he also perceives that the noumenon is central to all activity in the phenomenal world: it is around the still point that the world keeps turning. Under the aspect of eternity, therefore, the phenomenal world and the noumenon, the turning world and the still point are not at odds with each other.

The image of the wheel is first evoked by the Third Priest when he learns of the dubious peace surrounding Becket's return from exile: "For good or ill, let the wheel turn./ The wheel has been still, these seven years, and no good./ For ill or good, let the wheel turn" (*MC*, p. 243). Lacking a clear insight into the still point, the Third Priest can only perceive the procession of events in time; nor can he see whether Becket's return bodes good or evil. He is conscious only of the turning world; hence its real significance escapes him.

Far different is the perception of Thomas Becket; he intuitively grasps, even if he does not fully realize, the greater pattern implied by the still point. He is also conscious of the peace and harmony that attends a life lived by eternal principles. Hence, the very first word he utters is "Peace" (*MC*, p. 245). Then, he gently rebukes the Second Priest for deriding the superstitious fears of the women of Canterbury; they may be simple and ignorant, but Becket is aware that they too have a part to play in the eternal design:

> They know and do not know, what it is to act or suffer
> They know and do not know, that action is suffering
> And suffering is action. Neither does the agent suffer
> Nor the patient act. But both are fixed
> In an eternal action, an eternal patience
> To which all must consent that it may be willed
> And which all must suffer that they may will it,
> That the pattern may subsist, for the pattern is the action
> And the suffering, that the wheel may turn and still
> Be forever still. (*MC*, p. 245)

Becket's perception is awesome in its breadth and clarity. Life consists in action and to act is to be involved in suffering—or as Krishna and the Buddha put it, suffering is the fruit of *karma*. Acting and suffering, suffering and acting, therefore, all life turns on the wheel. Apparently this temporal existence is meaningless and futile, but action and suffering do have a significance from an eternal viewpoint, for they impel all life towards the still centre of the wheel. Moreover, the turning world has no reality apart from the still point; hence, there is neither suffering nor action in the eternal perspective.

Becket might almost be paraphrasing the philosophical concept cryptically expressed by Krishna to Arjuna in the *Gita*:

> If any man thinks he slays, and if another thinks he is slain,
> neither knows the ways of truth. The Eternal in man cannot
> kill: the Eternal in man cannot die. (2: 19)
>   Not by refraining from action does man attain freedom from

action. Not by mere renunciation does he attain supreme
perfection. (3: 4)
    Whatever you do, or eat, or give, or offer in adoration, let
it be an offering to me; and whatever you suffer, suffer for
me. (9: 27)[39]

This concept was first embodied in American poetry in "Brahma," a poem
Eliot surely knew, by Ralph Waldo Emerson:

> If the red slayer thinks he slays,
>   Or if the slain thinks he is slain,
> They know not well the subtle ways
>   I keep, and pass, and turn again.[40]

    Becket alludes to the wheel again when his First Tempter tries to lead him
astray from his responsibilities by recalling the pleasant carefree times of his
youth. Becket firmly refuses to return to his former way of life, for "Only/
The fool, fixed in his folly, may think/ He can turn the wheel on which he
turns" (*MC*, p. 247). Becket is no fool; he knows his past life cannot be
revived; he cannot turn back the wheel on which he is bound. He prefers to
free himself of his bondage by striving towards the central axis of the wheel.
    But his progress towards the centre is not without hazard. The Fourth
Tempter tempts him with his own innate desire for the martyrdom and glory
of the saints and troubles him with his own doubts regarding the eternal
design:

> You have also thought, sometimes at your prayers
> Sometimes hesitating at the angles of stairs,
> And between sleep and waking, early in the morning,
> When the bird cries, have thought of further scorning.
> That nothing lasts, but the wheel turns. (*MC*, p. 254)

The implication is clear: everything is ephemeral, in flux; hence, existence is
a meaningless sequence of action and suffering—a proposition Becket rejected
in his first speech. The Fourth Tempter does not give him time to collect his
thoughts; he proceeds, with great irony, to repeat Becket's earlier speech
word for word, so that Becket has his own sage reflections on the wheel and
its eternal significance flung in his teeth. Presumably, he learns a valuable
lesson: reality can only be realized in action; it can never be conveniently
encapsulated in words or thoughts. When he resists the temptation to do "the
right deed for the wrong reason" (*MC*, p. 258) and resolves to act in a spirit of
self-surrender, his course is clear: "I shall no longer act or suffer, to the

sword's end./ Now my good angel, whom God appoints/ To be my guardian, hover over the swords' points" (*MC*, p. 259). He is well on his way to the still centre of the wheel and peace.

In *The Family Reunion*, Harry knows as well as Becket that only the fool thinks "he can turn the wheel on which he turns" (*MC*, p. 247). He confesses to Agatha and others his one-time folly of trying to turn the wheel back and seek even a brief respite from suffering:

> One thinks to escape
> By violence, but one is still alone
> In an over-crowded desert, jostled by ghosts.
> It was only reversing the senseless direction
> For a momentary rest on *the burning wheel*
> That cloudless night in the mid-Atlantic
> When I pushed her over. (*FR*, p. 294)

He has now recognized his sickness; he holds at least "a fragment of the explanation" (*FR*, p. 296), and this, in turn, Agatha assures him, will eventually deepen his understanding and show "the way to freedom" (*FR*, p. 296).

Harry's other aunts and uncles, even his mother, inhabit the Waste Land, but they are mostly unaware of their spiritual condition. Harry's mother, Amy, for instance, sighs for the return of spring and youth; little does she know that "April is the cruellest month" (*WL*, p. 61), marking yet another beginning of the cycle of birth and death; nor does she pause to think, in her folly, that she cannot turn back the wheel on which she turns. Ivy, one of Harry's aunts, insists that if she were Amy, she "would go south in the winter" (*FR*, p. 285), unconsciously echoing the speaker in the opening section of *The Waste Land*. As for the others—Charles, with his country squire's tastes, Gerald, in his *pukka sahib*'s role, and Violet, with her *grande dame* attitudes— one and all, they are denizens of the Waste Land.

When Harry appears in their midst after several years' absence, they are all struck by his obvious distress over his spiritual condition; when he opens his mouth, he does not speak "their language" (*FR*, p. 324). These factors arouse a vague disquiet in their minds, so that when he leaves them for a while to take his bath, they have a sudden flash of insight into the general human predicament and chant in chorus: "We all of us make the pretension/ To be the uncommon exception/ To the universal bondage" (*FR*, p. 301). They experience the "horror" Kurtz perceived, but their moment of awareness is short-lived, and in the end they insist that the world is what they have always taken it to be—a safe and familiar place in which to drag out their pointless lives. Harry instinctively senses their spiritual bankruptcy soon after his return and identifies them accurately as "people/ To whom nothing has happened, at most a continual impact/ of external events. You have gone through life in sleep/ Never woken to the nightmare" (*FR*, p. 293). In fact, their condition is like that of the hollow men going round and round the prickly pear in the cactus land, a death-in-life. But Harry also knows that their lives would be unendurable if they were "wide awake" (*FR*, p. 293), since mankind cannot bear much reality.

Unlike his mother, Harry does not yearn for spring; on the contrary, he dislikes it. In his conversation with Mary, his childhood friend, he speaks of spring as "an evil time, that excites with lying voices" and identifies it with the resurrection of the dead:

> Spring is an issue of blood
> A season of sacrifice
> And the wail of the new full tide
> Returning the ghosts of the dead
> Those whom the winter drowned
> *Do not the ghosts* of the drowned
> *Return* to land in the spring?
> *Do the dead want to return?* (*FR*, p. 310; my emphasis)

Mary completes his thought:

> I believe the season of birth
> Is the season of sacrifice
> For the tree and the beast, and the fish
> Thrashing itself upstream:
> And what of *the terrified spirit*
> *Compelled to be reborn* . . . (*FR*, p. 310; my emphasis)

The implication is clear: spring is "an evil time," precisely because it portends reincarnation, which, in turn, means continuous bondage to the turning wheel. Both Harry and Mary recognize this significance, because both long to be free.

Later, Harry appeals to Agatha for help in finding a way out of his predicament because he has always imagined her to be strong and free. He discovers that she is actually a fellow-traveller on the path to freedom:

> I have thought of you as the completely strong,
> *The liberated from the human wheel.*
> So I looked to you for help. Now I think it is
> *A common pursuit of liberation.* (*FR*, p. 331; my emphasis)

So he tries to explore the past in her company and gain a clearer insight into reality. He finds his awareness deepening, so that he eloquently recaptures the momentary release he once obtained from bondage to the wheel:

> In and out, in *an endless drift*
> Of shrieking forms *in a circular desert*
> Weaving with contagion of putrescent embraces
> On dissolving bone. In and out, the movement
> *Until the chain broke*, and I was left
> Under the single eye above the desert. (*FR*, p. 335; my emphasis)

Agatha, who is also conscious of being enchained to the wheel, confirms Harry's intuition: each is a prisoner of the turning world "until the chain breaks" (*FR*, p. 335). Harry vents his feelings of frustration and despair over still leading an unredeemed life full of change and suffering:

> To and fro, dragging my feet
> Among inner shadows in the smoky wilderness,
> Trying to avoid the clasping branches
> And the giant lizard. To and fro.
> Until the chain breaks.
>   The chain breaks,
> The wheel stops. (*FR*, p. 335)

This is a climactic moment of revelation in Harry's life. Now he clearly understands the greater pattern of existence: only when the still centre is clearly perceived and firmly grasped does "the chain" break and "the wheel" stop, freeing man from all the phantasmagoria of the turning world. Immediately after his moment of revelation, the Furies, who have been pursuing Harry, appear before him. He is no longer afraid and is prepared to follow them, for he knows now that ultimately he will be cleansed of his imperfections and led to the still point.

Towards the end of *The Family Reunion*, when Harry has departed to follow the Eumenides, all the members of his family except Agatha and Mary are left in a sad state of bewilderment. Agatha and Mary, however, set up "a birthday cake with lighted candles" and "walk slowly in single file round and round the table, clockwise; at each revolution, they blow out a few candles, so that their last words are spoken in the dark" (*FR*, p. 349). It is a touching scene, reminiscent of the dignified and harmonious dance of the country people in "East Coker." The birthday cake might be said to symbolize the rebirth of the spirit in the divine order. Appropriately, Agatha's closing words are both a prayer and a benediction:

> This way the pilgrimage
> Of expiation
> Round and round the circle
> Completing the charm
> So the knot be unknotted
> The crossed be uncrossed. (*FR*, p. 350)

The darkness in which these words are spoken is not the darkness of ignorance; it is rather the knowledge of reality, which Vaughan described as the "dazzling darkness" of God.[41] It is a divine darkness that comes only when all actions are performed in a spirit of self-surrender, extinguishing all present and future incarnations, like the candles on the birthday cake.

Harry's consciousness of bondage to a "burning wheel" and a "human wheel" resembles Lear's when he declares that he is "bound/ Upon a wheel of fire."[42] Eliot knew these words well, especially since he wrote an introduction to G. Wilson Knight's *The Wheel of Fire*. He must also have been aware that the image of the wheel occurs through the ages in Christian writings, as, for example, in Dante and St. Augustine:

> To the high fantasy here power failed; but already my desire and will were rolled—even as the wheel that moveth quickly—by the Love that moves the sun and the stars.

> My will the enemy held, and thence had made a chain for me, and bound me. For a forward will was a lust made; and a lust served, became custome; and custom not resisted, became necessity. By which links, as it were, joined together (whence I called a chain) a hard bondage held me enthralled.[43]

However, the symbolism of the wheel in its universal aspects is found even more frequently in Hindu-Buddhist writings. Moreover, the Lama in *Kim* speaks of the wheel and its significance. Not surprisingly, therefore, the interior landscapes of both Agatha and Harry betray oriental overtones. Agatha speaks of moments of suffering which burn an individual "across a whole Thibet of broken stones" (*FR*, p.332), while Harry refers to "the worship in the desert, the thirst and deprivation,/ A stony sanctuary and a primitive altar" (*FR*, p.339). And both allude similarly to the freedom of the still point:

> Until the chain broke . . .
> Until the chain breaks . . .
> Until the chain breaks.
>   The chain breaks.
> The wheel stops. (*FR*, p. 335)

Where is the closest parallel to these words and images? Not in Dante, St. Augustine, or Shakespeare, nor even in an Upanishad or the *Gita*, but in Edwin Arnold's *The Light of Asia*, which Eliot read as a boy and never forgot. There the Buddha speaks graphically of release from change and suffering:

> If ye lay bound upon *the wheel of change*,
> And no way of *breaking from the chain*,
> The heart of boundless being is a curse,
> The soul of things, fell pain.
> ... Ye suffer from yourselves. None else compels
> ... you that live and die.
> and whirl upon *the wheel*. (my emphasis)[44]

No doubt, the mature Eliot vividly recalled Arnold's phrases and literally echoed them in *The Family Reunion*.

This does not necessarily mean that Dante, St. Augustine, and Shakespeare, not to mention the Hindu-Buddhist scriptures, are nowhere in the picture. Eliot probably amalgamated the ideas he had gleaned from reading these Western authors and Eastern texts with the strong impressions of his youth. After all, such an East-West ideosynthesis was not alien to his temperament. Had he not already practised it dramatically by collocating the Buddha and St. Augustine together at the very core of *The Waste Land*?

The image of the wheel does not occur in *The Cocktail Party*, *The Confidential Clerk*, and *The Elder Statesman*, but the associated bondage does manifest itself in the lives of the characters in these plays. Edward and Lavinia, Peter and Celia in *The Cocktail Party*, Sir Claude and Colby in *The Confidential Clerk*, Lord Claverton, Charles, and Monica in *The Elder Statesman* are all at first very much embroiled in their own affairs, so that they may well be thought of as being chained to the wheel. By the end, however, they have all gained wisdom. The progress of Celia and Lord Claverton towards the still point is particularly rapid: Celia becomes a missionary and dies a martyr like Becket, while Lord Claverton gives up all pretence, dies to his old self, and is consequently "brushed by the wing of happiness" (*ES*, p. 581).

Even in his most 'Christian' writing, the modern 'Mystery' play *The Rock*, Eliot evokes the wheel at the beginning:

> O perpetual revolution of configured stars,
> O perpetual recurrence of determined seasons,
> O world of spring and autumn, birth and dying!
> The endless cycle of idea and action,

Endless invention, endless experiment,
Brings knowledge of motion, but not of stillness;
Knowledge of speech, but not of silence;
Knowledge of words, and ignorance of the Word. (*CR*, p. 147)

The concepts of impermanence and suffering, the ceaseless flux of existence, the endless cycle of birth and death, the turning world and the still point are all clearly and succinctly expressed here. It is the nearest Eliot ever comes to a complete elucidation of the symbolism of the wheel.

"The deeper design," then, as Eliot writes elsewhere,[45] "is that of human misery and bondage which is universal," though the individual *can* liberate himself from the wheel of *saṁsāra* and attain the peace of the still centre. Nevertheless, there is this question: what prevents the individual bound on the turning wheel of the phenomenal world from an immediate perception of the still point? The answer lies in the source of suffering and the mysterious phenomenon known as *māyā*.

3

CRAVING AND MĀYĀ

Mirror upon mirror mirrored is all the show.
                                        W.B. YEATS
The cloud-capped tow'rs, the gorgeous palaces,
The solemn temples, the great globe itself,
Yea, all which it inherit, shall dissolve,
And, like this insubstantial pageant faded,
Leave not a rack behind. We are such stuff
As dreams are made on.
                        SHAKESPEARE, *The Tempest*

Flux and suffering are inseparable from existence in the phenomenal world. People change with time, act and remember, weep and smile, but the agony abides and even the laughter in the rose garden points before and after to the agony of birth and death. The cause of such suffering is craving. In the *Gita*, Krishna tells Arjuna:

> All is clouded in desire; as the fire by smoke, as a mirror by dust, as an unborn babe by its covering.
>   Wisdom is clouded by desire, the everpresent enemy of the wise, desire in its innumerable forms, which like a fire cannot find satisfaction.[1]

The same truth is revealed by the Buddha to his monks in his first sermon in the Deer Park:

> The Noble Truth of the origin of suffering, O monks, is this: it is this thirst (craving) which produces re-existence and re-becoming, bound up with passionate greed. It finds fresh delight now here and now there,

namely, thirst for sense pleasures; thirst for existence and becoming; and thirst for non-existence (self-annihilation).[2]

This thirst (*taṇhā*) for life or craving for the transient things of this phenomenal world is explicitly discouraged by Christ too in the Gospels.

The characters in Eliot's early poems incessantly crave sensual gratification, which breeds attachment to ephemeral things in them. Consequently, their craving or thirst is never satisfied and their lives are full of suffering.

Prufrock, for instance, drags out a maimed and crippled existence, tormented by unappeasable desires. An aging and inhibited dreamer, imprisoned by his shabby genteel environment, he is obsessed by the spectacle of lust around him:

> And I have known the arms already, known them all—
> Arms that are braceleted and white and bare
> (But in the lamplight, downed with light brown hair!)
> Is it perfume from a dress
> That makes me so digress?
> Arms that lie along a table, or wrap about a shawl. (LP, p.15)

Yet he lacks the courage to break out of his mould; he dare not "disturb the universe" and ask a lady at a party "the overwhelming question" (LP, p. 15) for that would upset the comfortable pattern of his "civilized" life. At the end of the poem, it is certain that Prufrock will continue to circulate in the drawing rooms where "women come and go talking of Michelangelo" and that he will continue to measure out his life with "coffee spoons," a prey to conflicting desires (LP, p. 14). In short, he has resigned himself to bondage on the wheel.

Presumably, this is the common lot of the inhabitants of the world displayed in the poems that succeed "Prufrock." The young man in "Portrait of a Lady" commits "a psychological rape" by "penetrating to the depths of the lady's lonely and empty life,"[3] while she, aware that life and youth are slipping away, clings pathetically to his companionship in the hope that it might develop into something deeper. Mr. Apollinax, who laughs like "an irresponsible foetus" at polite society, is a shocking sensualist (MA, p. 31). Apeneck Sweeney, who knows "the female temperament," loves to flaunt his body, "pink from nape to base," and spends his time guarding "the horned gate" (SE, p. 42, SAN, p.56). Grishkin tempts men to seize, clutch and penetrate sensual experience: "Uncorseted, her friendly bust/ Gives promise of pneumatic bliss" (WI, p. 52). Burbank is aware of literary and artistic values apart from his Baedeker, but this knowledge does not prevent him from succumbing to the charms of Princess Volupine. One and all, they are chained to the wheel, whirled about by shifting desires.

Gerontion contrasts the secular history of mankind, of which his own life forms a tiny part, with the ignored promise of redemption through a man-God like Christ (or Krishna or the Buddha). He symbolizes civilization gone rotten. His thoughts are peopled by frustrated society ladies, corrupt financiers, and decayed nobility, who lead lives of quiet desperation full of debauchery and self-indulgence. What he describes is "the unstilled world" (*AW*, p. 96)—to borrow a phrase from *Ash Wednesday*—the turning wheel and not the still point where lust perishes and love fructifies into compassion. Gerontion realizes that man cannot but split into "fractured atoms" (G, p. 39) in the flux of history and that permanence resides only at the still centre, now "Swaddled with darkness" (G, p. 37). He himself has not attained the still point, for though he has lost the "passion" of his youth, he has not outgrown the memories of that passion. His thoughts still have the power to "Excite the membrane, when the sense has cooled,/ With pungent sauces" (G, p. 38). Consequently, he continues to be bound to the wheel, whose horror he perceives but cannot escape.

At the very core of *The Waste Land*, in the section called "The Fire Sermon," the Buddha and St. Augustine are brought together. Like the original Fire Sermon of the Buddha, the poem deals with human bondage resulting from lust for the transitory things of this world. Eliot extends the principle expounded by the Buddha and marshals the Buddha and St. Augustine—and implicitly Christ and the Upanishadic sages—as an "army of unalterable law" (CN, p. 30) against the Sweeneys and Mrs. Porters of this world. Though the Buddha and St. Augustine are separated by time and space, they *are* united in Tiresias' consciousness and share a common concern: to trace the origin of suffering. They conclude that it springs from craving or thirst for the love of created things; both use fire as a symbol of the craving that devours man, binds him to the turning world, and prevents him from attaining *nirvanā* or union with the divine essence. This craving or *taṇhā*, in its widest sense, stands for that persistent clinging to present existence and incessant longing for future existence which animates all beings in the phenomenal world. It is repeatedly associated with lust in the poem, lust which Shakespeare describes as the "expense of spirit in a waste of shame." It is the lust of the barbarous king which rudely forces Philomela to a lower turn of the wheel and changes her into a nightingale; it is lust which brings Sweeney to Mrs. Porter in the spring and the carbuncular young man to the typist over the unlit stairs; it is lust which forms the topic of conversation among the working-class women in the pub and the theme of the song of the violated Thames daughters. Invariably, it brings suffering in its wake.

The symbolism of the wheel is interwoven with the theme of craving throughout the poem to represent a vivid picture of pain and suffering. Flux, suffering, and craving are all projected through a complex image of joyless spring at the beginning of the poem: April is "the cruellest month" (*WL*, p. 61) precisely because it mixes the "memory" of former existences in dead cities with the "desire" (craving or *taṇha*) for evanescent things and causes the wheel to revolve, chaining mankind to the endless cycle of reincarnation and suffering.

The figurative straw dummies shuffling despondently round the prickly pear in *The Hollow Men* are inheritors of the desolation of the Waste Land. They cannot assert their freedom by spiritual or moral choice; rather, they are content to merely gratify their most immediate needs. The prickly pear is a phallic symbol denoting lust. It is substituted for the mulberry bush—a fertility symbol denoting love, according to Grover Smith[5]—in the parody of the nursery rhyme chanted by the hollow men. Consequently, their dance represents an absorption with sexuality that excludes the still centre. Their spiritually sterile condition is reflected by their desert environment, wherein their thirst for sensual gratification can never be allayed but can only scorch their hearts with agony:

> In death's other kingdom
> Waking alone
> At the hour when we are
> Trembling with tenderness
> Lips that would kiss
> Form prayers to broken stone. (*HM*, p. 84)

In short, the hollow men inhabit a nightmarish world in which their desires involve them in continual suffering.

The spiritual distress of the protagonist of *Ash Wednesday* resembles that of the wastelanders and the hollow men; unlike them, however, he is aware of the cause of his suffering and is determined to remove it. He knows from the start what Tiresias does not learn till the end and what the wastelanders and the hollow men never learn: the quest for the peace and certitude of the still point is possible only through the renunciation of desire for the transient pleasures of the turning world. The poem, begins, therefore, with the protagonist's fervent wish to give up desires and be free of turning on the wheel:

> Because I do not hope to turn again
> Because I do not hope
> Because I do not hope to turn
> Desiring this man's gift and that man's scope
> I no longer strive towards such things. (*AW*, p. 89)

But he finds that it is not easy to relinquish attachment "to self and to things and to persons" (LG, p. 195) and to cultivate detachment from the turning world. The human will is susceptible and is always capable of turning back to the temptations from which it has turned away. Thus, even while he is advancing towards the still centre, the protagonist cannot avoid a backward glance:

> At the first turning of the second stair
> I turned and saw below
> The same shape twisted on the banister
> Under the vapour in the fetid air
> Struggling with the devil of the stairs who wears
> The deceitful face of hope and despair. (AW, p. 93)

The worst struggle is past, but it is so recent that he cannot forget it. As long as memory persists, he has not entirely vanquished desire. "The devil of the stairs" stands in his thought for the temptations of the turning world, which provoke false hope and its related despair, temptations which undermine the detachment he prays for. But detachment does not mean indifference. Indifference is callous unconcern for the suffering of fellow beings. Detachment is freedom from egotistic self-seeking, a condition attainable by those whose selfish desires have been consumed in the fire of God's love, so that they are compassionate towards all suffering beings and do them selfless service. When this detachment is not present, man is still prey to the thirst (taṇhā) for sensual gratification and participates in the vanity fair of "the unstilled world" (AW, p. 96), whose movement is apparently contradictory to the silent Word.

This "unstilled world" is vividly described in the third section of "Burnt Norton" as "a place of disaffection/ Time before and time after/ In a dim light" (BN, p. 173). "Disaffection" stands for indifference or "tumid apathy" towards the sufferings of others. This indifference, no less than attachment to the transient beauties and pleasures of the phenomenal world, confines man to the wheel's "slow rotation" (BN, p. 173). Apathy brutalizes and stupefies most human beings so that they become hollow men and inhabit the cactus land. And because of them, the turning world appears to be in opposition to the still point.

The seemingly contradictory movement of the "unstilled world" in time is comparable to the confined motion of a train on its rails: "the world moves/ In appetency, on its metalled ways/ Of time past and time future" (BN, p. 174). Appetency is that which impels man to cling on to present existence and to yearn for its continuation. This appetency, in the form of will to live against all odds, is repeatedly associated with the approach of spring in

Eliot's poetry, but with overtones of pain. For instance, in "East Coker," craving and pain are projected through a complex image of spring out of season, wherein birth is aborted and hopes of life are crushed:

> What is the late November doing
> With the disturbance of the spring
> And creatures of the summer heat
> And snowdrops writhing under feet
> And hollyhocks that aim too high
> Red into grey and tumble down
> Late roses filled with early snow? (EC, p. 178)

This unnatural conduct of the seasons represents the disorder of the human spirit that results when earthly desires are given free rein, because "Desire itself is movement/ Not in itself desirable" (BN, p. 175), binding man down to the flux of the turning world and causing him unending anxiety and misery. In other words, desire confines man to the circumference of the wheel, clots "the bedded axle-tree" (BN, p. 172), and prevents him from attaining the still centre, which alone can impart "The inner freedom from the practical desires,/ The release from action and suffering, release from the inner/ And outer compulsion" (BN, p. 173).

In *Murder in the Cathedral*, Becket knows that desire or craving for the gratifications of the phenomenal world is a major impediment to the apprehension of the still point. His Four Tempters try to deflect him from his purpose by confronting him with desire in various forms. He summarily dismisses the temptations of worldly pleasure, of power (through subservience to the king), and of influence (through alliance with the barons). The Fourth Tempter proves almost too much for him; as Becket admits, the Fourth Tempter tempts him with his own "desires," his own dreams of "eternal grandeur," of an "enduring crown" to be won through martyrdom (*MC*, p.255). He realizes, however, that in consciously willing himself to martyrdom he is arrogating to himself the powers of God. Finally, he renounces his desire and humbly resigns himself to the task of "making perfect his will" (*MC*, p. 271) to fit the divine purpose.

In *The Family Reunion*, Harry is aware that he is bound on the "burning wheel" of memory and desire, from which he seeks escape by violence (*FR*, p. 294), pushing his wife overboard in mid-Atlantic. But his suffering is augmented, not reduced, by his violent action; his past haunts him and creates a nightmarish present in which he keeps moving "In and out, in an endless drift/ Of shrieking forms in a circular desert" (*FR*, p. 335). However, he comes to understand through Agatha that it is possible to transcend despair and that suffering can be a means of purgation. He learns to accept that "the past is irremediable" and that "the future can only be built/ Upon the real past" (*FR*, p. 336). Brooding on or struggling against the present and future consequences of the past is vain and cannot free him from time and circumstance. On the other hand, acceptance of "what can't be got rid of" makes him quite content, for it brings him what Agatha calls "relief"— "relief from what had happened/ Is also relief from that *unfulfilled craving/* Flattered in sleep and deceived in waking" (*FR*, p. 336; my emphasis). Recovering his sanity, he starts to believe like Agatha that the flux can be overcome and the turns of the wheel stilled. This insight into the nature of existence marks the beginning of Harry's "pursuit of liberation" (*FR*, p. 331). Urged on by Agatha and by the promptings of his inner self, he declines to settle down as his mother wishes to a safe and comfortable life in his ancestral home; instead, he chooses the self-sacrificing life of a missionary in a harsh environment among humble people.

The Cocktail Party deals with the frustration and despair in male-female relationships when there is only desire and not love. Edward and Lavinia are married, but they are incapable of loving each other. Lavinia has an extra-marital relationship with Peter, a young filmwriter who thinks he is in love with Celia. Celia, in turn, is Edward's mistress. All lead empty lives and suffer acutely but do not know why. When they discover the root cause of their suffering to be attachment "to self and to things and to persons" (*LG*, p. 195), they modify their lives, according to the prescription of Sir Henry Harcourt-Reilly, an analytical psychologist. Edward and Lavinia find that they share the same isolation because they are really in love with themselves. Lacking knowledge of the still point, they do not recognize their dependence on God; hence, their act of loving does not reflect their love for the creator, and their relationship leads to mutual disillusionment and despair. Narcis-sistically, they see in each other's face only a reflection of their own selfish needs. Or, as Sir Henry points out, they carry with them "the shadow of desires of desires" (*CP*, p. 410). They occupy the periphery of the turning wheel and share the centrifugal motion of the damned. All that they can do is to follow Sir Henry's advice and make "the best of a bad job" (*CP*, p. 410). Their only consolation is that they know themselves to be what they are—"A man who finds himself incapable of loving/ And a woman who finds that no man can love her" (*CP*, p. 410). This self-knowledge they have in common is a bond that holds them together while they are "still in a state of unenlightenment" (*CP*, p. 410), unaware of the nature of the Buddhahood or the still point. Celia discovers that she had not really loved Edward when she had been his mistress; she had merely been in love with an image of her own needs:

The man I saw before, he was only a projection—
I see that now—of something I wanted—
No, not *wanted*—something I aspired to—
Something I desperately wanted to exist. (*CP*, p. 382)

Her honesty compels Edward to recognize that he had never loved her, only desired her, and that now he has lost even the "desire for all that was most desirable" (*CP*, p. 381). Whereas Edward's growing self-awareness leads him to a reconciliation with Lavinia, Celia's self-knowledge intensifies her quest for peace. She too seeks Sir Henry's counsel, wanting "to be cured/ Of a *craving* for something I cannot find/ And of the shame of never finding it" (*CP*, p. 417; my emphasis). Her craving, however, is no longer for the transitory pleasures of the phenomenal world; she now yearns for the love of God. Under Sir Henry's guidance, she chooses the lonely way of the contemplative mystic that finally leads her, like Becket, to martyrdom. After Celia's death by crucifixion in the missionary outpost of Kinkanja, Peter learns through Lavinia that he too did not love Celia; he had been deluded by his own desires; "What you've been living on is an image of Celia/ Which you made for yourself, to meet your own needs" (*CP*, p. 435). He recognizes this as true. Sobered by this self-knowledge and with the memory of Celia's self-sacrifice, he resumes his artistic career. Though still bound to the turning wheel, he is now aware of the existence of the still point and of the selfish desires that make him suffer by obscuring it.

The Confidential Clerk provides a dramatic illustration of the emptiness that ensues when a man devotes himself to a career in the world of art or business, without knowing that a centre exists. Sir Claude has given up his dream of being a potter to become a businessman, but he finds himself living in a world of "make-believe" (*CC*, p. 466), from which he periodically escapes by retreating to a room containing his china and porcelain creations. These *objets d'art* enable him occasionally to enter a "real world" in which he experiences "that sense of identification/ With the maker . . . —an agonising ecstasy/ Which makes life bearable" (*CC*, p. 466). But he lacks the strength to commit himself wholeheartedly to art and to act as an instrument of the divine purpose. He is not a good businessman either, since he does not share his father's passion for business. Since he has built his life on self-deception, his attempts to find an outlet for his frustration through his love for his illegitimate son, Colby, are also thwarted. Consequently, he has only his potter's creations to live by, attachments that do not culminate in the love of God and his fellow beings. They only bind him ever more firmly to the turning world and prolong his agony. Colby too has relinquished his ideal of being a great organist to become his father's confidential clerk. From time to time he too withdraws into the "secret world," as his half-sister Lucasta calls it, of his "inner garden" (*CC*, p. 472), but Colby cannot rest content with a part-time consolation. He knows that he has to make both his inner and outer life meaningful; he has to choose between a life of divided loyalties and a life of singlemindedness that reaches toward the still point. Colby is finally incapable of making such an existential choice. He welcomes an opportunity to work as a church organist, but he does not want to make spiritual capital out of sacred music and become a priest. In the end, therefore, Sir Claude and Colby are still bound to the wheel, wallowing in the welter of their attachments "to self and to things and to persons" (*LG*, p. 195).

In *The Elder Statesman*, Lord Claverton is forced step-by-step to strip himself of his false masks as distinguished administrator, irreproachable father and faithful husband and to accept the truth about his real nature. Confronted by a former friend and mistress—he calls them "Spectres from my past" (*ES*, p. 569)—who accuse him of having corrupted their nature and violated their love, he is compelled to recognize that he has spent his life exploiting others in order to gratify his selfish desires for power and pride. He confesses his errors to Charles and Monica and thus takes "the first step" towards his "freedom" (*ES*, p. 572). He decides to turn and confront his spectres, enduring the humiliation and suffering inherent in his past attachment "to self and to things and to persons" (*LG*, p. 195). However, he finds himself a helpless spectator when his "spectres" lure his son, Michael, away to a corrupt life at San Marco. Knowing that he has paved his son's way to turpitude by setting a bad example, Lord Claverton accepts Michael's repudiation of his former existence:

> And Michael—
> I love him, even for rejecting me,
> For the *me* he rejected, I reject also.
> I've been freed from the self that pretends to be someone;
> And in becoming no one, I begin to live. (*ES*, p. 582)

He realizes that he has always dominated his children, so that he could fulfil his desires through them and believe in his "pretences." He dies to his false self and is reborn as "the man he really is." Having understood his past and repudiated the craving (*taṇhā*) for the perpetuation of his pretentious self, he attains peace and is "brushed by the wing of happiness" (*ES*, p. 581).

Craving and its consequent suffering, then, are as intrinsic to the universal design for Eliot as for Krishna, the Buddha, and Christ. To be a slave of shifting desires, without realizing that they give birth to endless suffering, is to be blindly caught up in the revolutions of the wheel; it is *avidyā* or ignorance. Not to seek a way out of this bondage is to be lost in the darkness of *māyā* or the world of appearances.

The term *māyā* has a long history in Indian philosophy. In the *Rig Veda*, it denotes a mysterious deceptive power of the gods. In the Upanishads, the Lord wields *māyā* to project Nature (*prākriti*) and to conjure up the world of appearances. Nature, then, is the manifestation of the Lord's creative power, his *māyā*, and Nature can delude man when he takes it to be an independent ultimate reality. Thus, we read in the *Svetasvatara Upanishad*:

> For all the sacred books, all holy sacrifice and ritual and prayers, all the words of the Vedas, and the whole past and present and future, come from the Spirit. With Maya, his power of wonder, he made all things, and by Maya the human soul is bound.
>
> Know therefore that nature is Maya, but that God is the ruler of Maya; and that all beings in our universe are parts of his infinite splendour.[6]

The *Gita* deals even more emphatically with the same concept:

> Helpless all, for Māyā is their master,
> And I, their Lord, the master of this Māyā . . .
> Māyā makes all things: what moves, what is unmoving.
> O son of Kunti, that is why the world spins,
> Turning its wheel through birth
> And through destruction.[7]

The concept of *māyā* flowers most completely in the non-dualistic (*advaita*) Vedanta of the eighth-century philosopher, Sankara, who revived the Hindu way of life by reinforcing the non-dual reality (*Brahman*) of the Upanishads and the *Gita*. According to *advaita,* our perception of an independent material world of objects, persons, and processes is grounded in a pervasive error. We take the unreal for real and the real for unreal. This is borne out by the famous analogy of the snake and rope. We often *mis*-take a coil of rope for a snake in the dark; but, on closer examination, we discover it to be only a coil of rope. Our everyday world of appearances may be likened to a snake, and it seems very real to us; we are in the darkness of ignorance, caught in the web of illusion. When we are illumined, we experience the truth; the snake-appearance vanishes into the underlying reality of the rope. This does not mean that the world of appearances is non-existent; the world, according to Sankara, "is and is not."[8] When we are in a state of ignorance, our everyday consciousness experiences the world, and it exists as it appears; in the dark, the snake appears real. When we are enlightened and pass into a transcendental consciousness, the world ceases to exist; the snake disappears and the rope alone is real. Thus, we are confronted by a paradox— the world is and the world is not. It is neither real nor non-existent. Yet this apparent paradox is simply a statement of fact—a fact which Sankara calls *māyā*. This *māyā*, this world-appearance, has its basis in *Brahman*, the one indivisible unchanging reality; and *māyā* not only conceals reality, but also distorts it. *Brahman* remains eternally infinite and unchanged. It is not transformed into the world. It simply *appears* as this world to us in our ignorance. Not only do we fail to perceive reality, but we also superimpose a snake upon a coil of rope in the dark. In short, we substitute a phenomenal world for the noumenon and take the unreal for real and the real for unreal; we are subject to *māyā*, the world-appearance. *Māyā* is characterized as beginningless (*anạdi*), since time occurs only within it; as unthinkable (*açintya*), for all thought is subject to it; as indescribable (*anirvaçanīya*), for all conceptual language results from it. To seek to know what causes *māyā* is to go beyond it—and when we do that, *māyā* vanishes like a mirage, for the effect ceases to exist, and there is only *Brahman*, the one unchanging reality. So Sankara concludes:

> The universe does not exist apart from *Brahman*. Our perception of it as having an independent existence is false, like our perception of blueness in the sky. How can a superimposed attribute have any existence, apart from its substratum? It is only our delusion which causes this mis-conception of the underlying reality.[9]

No matter what we think we are perceiving in our delusion, we are really seeing *Brahman* and nothing else but *Brahman*; only, we are not aware of this in our ignorance. We see a coil of rope and imagine it to be a snake; we see mother-of-pearl and imagine it to be silver; we see *Brahman* and imagine it to be the world.

Sankara's concept of *māyā* and *Brahman* is analogous to Bradley's theory of appearance and reality, on which Eliot write his doctoral dissertation. Staffan Bergsten comments interestingly:

> Long after he had finished his academic study of Bradley, Eliot wrote an essay on him which suggests his appreciation of the semi-religious metaphysician rather than the logician. The religious element underlying Bradley's concept of the Absolute had been noticed before, and it is significant that his philosophy has been compared with Vedic philosophy—as the bewildering illusions of Maya are brought to harmony in Brahman, so are appearances in reality.[10]

At the very outset of his *magnum opus, Appearance and Reality*, Bradley declares that his work will demonstrate the fact that the world "contradicts itself; and is, therefore, appearance, and not reality."[11] He scrutinizes the basic ideas and intellectual formulae through which man attempts to solve the riddle of the universe, such as motion and change, space, time and causation, and self and shows that they are all riddled with contradictions and do not comprise the whole truth. He concludes that the finite human experience of the world is not the experience of reality *as* reality, though it is the experience *of* reality. What is given to finite human experience, therefore, is not reality *qua* reality, but only a world of appearances; and yet, "there is reality in every appearance however slight."[12] In short, reality is inexplicably distorted into self-contradictory appearances: "The fact of appearance, and of the diversity of its particular spheres, we found was inexplicable, Why there are appearances, and why appearances of such various kinds, are questions not to be answered."[13] This inexplicable fact of world-appearance is precisely what Sankara calls *māyā*.

Bradley differs on one crucial point from Sankara, however. According to Bradley, reality *as* reality (that which is, the noumenon) cannot be experienced. He writes:

Fully to realize the existence of the Absolute is for finite beings impossible. In order thus to know we should have to be, and then *we* should not exist . . . . But to gain an idea of its main features . . . is a different endeavour. And it is a task in which we may succeed.[14]

Unlike Bradley, Sankara maintains that *Brahman* (or reality *qua* reality) can be concretely experienced and that, in experiencing it, we cease to exist as separate individuals. In other words, our individuality or ego is the result of our ignorance (*avidyā*) and is part of the world-appearance (*māyā*). When enlightenment comes, it is destroyed in the light of pure being that is *Brahman*, and we attain *nirvāna* or freedom from the bondage of the wheel of *samsāra*. Sankara's assertion that the ultimate reality of *Brahman* can be concretely experienced is in consonance with the teachings of the Upanishads and the *Gita*.

Eliot does uphold the possibility of attaining the reality of the still point, the silent centre around which all the world turns. He even goes so far as to say that most of us are vouchsafed "hints and guesses" (DS, p. 190) about the nature of the ultimate reality, though we are often incapable of the total apprehension possible to a saint. He seems, therefore, to have inclined more towards the vision (*darśana*) of ultimate reality enshrined in the Upanishads, the *Gita*, and the non-dualistic (*advaita*) Vedanta of Sankara than towards the agnosticism of Bradley. Moreover, the Christian writers Eliot drew upon—St. Augustine, St. John of the Cross, Dante, and Lancelot Andrewes— are all unequivocal in declaring that it is possible to be united with the divine essence. Consequently, in his poetic evocation of the multiple facets of the turning world and its unreality in the light of the still point, Eliot seems to have amalgamated what Bradley calls the inexplicable fact of world-appearance with what Sankara, following the Upanishads and the *Gita*, calls *māyā*.

Thus, the characters in Eliot's early poems may all be seen to be subject to *māyā*, deluded by the world of appearances. Prufrock's existence, as we saw earlier, is literally and metaphorically enveloped in a fog of unreality. He is conscious of having wasted his time in futile pursuits of self-gratification, of having measured out his life "with coffee spoons" (LP, p. 14). He cannot bring himself to ask his lady "the overwhelming question" (LP, p. 15), for that would destroy the comfortable illusion of his ordered world. He yearns to escape from his meaningless crippled existence, but his impulse to freedom lacks focus, so that he takes refuge in his dream-world of singing mermaids. He finds that he cannot even pinpoint the source of his anguish: "It is impossible to say just what I mean!/ But as if a magic lantern threw the nerves in patterns on a screen" (LP, p. 16). This is an inadvertent yet precise echo of Sankara's definition of *māyā*: it cannot be described, for all words and thoughts are its direct outcome. Prufrock's world, in short, has only an apparent reality, like the "patterns on a screen," and when he gropes for words to describe his existential situation or to indicate the nameless something he yearns for, he finds himself helpless and frustrated, reduced to shadow-boxing with reality.

The "Preludes" are unified by images which lend an air of unreality to varied scenes and actors. The first poem begins with winter nightfall in an urban backstreet and moves from the indoor gloom and the confined odour of cooking to the smoky twilight outside, in which the wind whips up the withered leaves and soiled newspapers and the raindrops spatter the housetops. The second poem reviews the street, as morning "comes to consciousness" of "faint stale smells of beer" and coffee fumes, like a person who has been out drinking all night and wakes up with a hangover. The poem ends contemplating the house windows, where innumerable hands raise "the dingy shades" to reveal "the other masquerades/ That time resumes" (P, p. 22). The third poem peeps into one of the "thousand furnished rooms" in which a rather filthy woman shakes off sleep and sluggishly tries to get out of bed; she has spent the night enthralled by the "thousand sordid images" (P, p. 23) of her soul flickering "against the ceiling" and now struggles to regain her day-to-day consciousness in order to resume her role in life's masquerade. The "sordid images" of her soul are comparable to the transitory show of fingers, pipes, newspapers, and eyes that constitute the soul of the personified street in the fourth poem. In other words, woman and street are both mere congeries of fugitive appearances; both are earthbound, she supine in her bed and "he" trampled by insistent feet. Nevertheless, both are vaguely aware of a hidden reality behind the apparent purposelessness of their existence; instinctively, their aspirations tend heavenward as they strive to free themselves; her soul's "images" flicker overhead, while "his" soul is "stretched tight across the skies" (P, p. 23). The "images" of the woman's soul and the passing show of the street mask reality from their consciousness. They are bedevilled by *māya*. Consequently, their struggle upward is blind and seems endless; so, their only hope lies in turning to the notion "of some infinitely gentle/ Infinitely suffering thing" (P, p. 23), of a compassionate Buddha or Christ figure who can help suffering humanity penetrate the veil of *māya* and attain the reality beyond appearances.

The consciousness of the protagonist of "Rhapsody on a Windy Night" resembles that of the woman in the "Preludes," for it imposes a subjective pattern on the kaleidoscopic images that meet his eyes, so that he too has "a vision of the street." Each street lamp he passes on his midnight ramble seems to beat like a "fatalistic drum," murmuring "lunar incantations" (RWN, p. 24), which combine with his latent memories to make up the rhapsody of his consciousness. The images that invade and possess his consciousness are all depressing and indicate the apparent meaninglessness of the universe. In fact, these images constitute his soul; he can no more escape the bleak landscape conjured up by his imagination than the woman of the "Preludes" can avoid the sordid pattern traced on her ceiling by her dreams. Even as he retreats into the solitude of his bedroom, the last street lamp lights his way up the stairs and reminds him that his *memory* has the key to free him from life's prison — the memory of a hidden reality, of that which is, behind life's masquerade. Nevertheless, memory alone is not enough; human effort is required to rend the veil of *māya*. Lacking the energy for this effort, the protagonist feels trapped; he is overcome by terror as the knowledge of his powerlessness to emancipate himself pierces him with a "last twist of the knife" (RWN, p. 26).

Gerontion is a logical extension of the nameless protagonist of "Rhapsody." As he squats outside his "decayed house," an old man driven to "a sleepy corner" (G, p. 39) to await his death, his mind is full of memories. He is acutely conscious of the futility of a world in which man stumbles down the "contrived corridors" of history (G, p. 38), lured by vanity and deceived by success, reluctant to choose "Christ the tiger" above sensual gratification — the futility of a maze whose centre man can no longer find. Gerontion himself cannot reach it; like his corrupt foreign acquaintances, he must share the centrifugal motion of the damned. He has lost the passion for earthly pleasures in his old age, but passion is strongest in memory and his sensual thoughts still have the power to "Excite the membrane, when the sense has cooled,/ With pungent sauces, multiply variety/ In a wilderness of mirrors" (G, p. 38). The unity behind the diversity of these mirror images is hidden from him; *māya* holds him yet in its relentless grip, distorting and concealing reality by its multitudinous appearances.

The modern figure of Gerontion is replaced by the mythological one of Tiresias to unify the diversities of *The Waste Land*.[15] Tiresias is more shadowy than Gerontion, so that most of the incidents in the poem seem immediate, not recalled, even though they are his memories. The disorganized flow of past events in his consciousness is so vivid and arresting that these events become present. In short, Tiresias *relives* his memories, as Kurtz does in Conrad's story, witnessing all his past lives "in every detail of desire, temptation and surrender."[16] "What Tiresias *sees*," therefore, "is the substance of the poem" (*WL*, p. 78)—a collage of images, mystifying statements, and dramatic encounters superimposed by his own mind on the basic substratum of reality.

It is perhaps instructive at this point to quote Sri Ramana Maharishi, one of the greatest modern exponents of the philosophy of non-duality (*advaita vedanta*) on *māyā*. Sri Ramana is not an academic theoretician, but a seer, in the living tradition of the Upanishadic sages. He speaks, therefore, simply and clearly, with the authority of one who knows from personal experience:

> You see various scenes passing on a cinema screen; fire seems to burn buildings to ashes; water seems to wreck ships; but the screen on which the pictures are projected remains unburnt and dry. Why? Because the pictures are unreal and the screen real. Similarly, reflections pass through a mirror but it is not affected at all by their number and quality.
>
> In the same way, the world is a phenomenon upon the substratum of the single Reality which is not affected by it in any way. Reality is only One. . . .
>
> Being now immersed in the world, you see it as a real world; get beyond it and it will disappear and Reality alone will remain.[17]

This might be a summing up of "what Tiresias *sees*" in *The Waste Land*. He is an uncommon spectator though, unlike most of mankind who are so immersed in the "passing show" that they fail to recognize it as mere appearance. He is conscious that the other characters, their words and deeds are fused together in his consciousness to form the subject of his reveries: "I Tiresias, old man with wrinkled dugs,/ Perceived the scene, foretold all the rest— .../ And I Tiresias have foresuffered all ...)" (*WL*, pp. 68-69). His consciousness may be described in the words of Bradley, which Eliot quoted in his notes to *The Waste Land*: it forms "a circle closed on the outside," a private world peopled by appearances (*WL*, p. 80). Curiously, he is not only a spectator of the gyrations of life within the maze of his consciousness, but also a participant in the past actions he recalls. He participates as "I Tiresias" in such flashback scenes as the fortune-telling of Madame Sosostris, the fornication of the typist with the carbuncular young man, and the journey across the desert to where the thunder is heard. Simultaneously, as spectator, he watches himself take part in the "passing show." He is the dreaming Alice of the Waste Land, who vividly recalls the episodes in which he figured prominently. Throughout the poem, he functions as a chorus, synthesizing and commenting on the actions of all who inhabit his dream, including himself. He perceives that neither the actors nor their deeds partake of the ultimate reality; they are all mere shadows, insubstantial as a dream. He does not use the word *māyā* when he sums up these appearances; he prefers the word "unreal." Thus, London and its crowds have only an apparent existence: "Unreal city/ Under the brown fog of a winter noon" (*WL*, p. 62). And because of the turns of the wheel, the ups and downs of history are cyclical; what is true of London is true of "Jerusalem Athens Alexandria/ Vienna" (*WL*, p. 73). The Jewish, Greek, and Egyptian civilizations have all declined; presumably, the European civilizations will follow. Those who inhabit these cities, the centres of modern civilization, are all (as the allusion to Baudelaire makes clear) ghosts of former lives, enacting the same roles again and again: "You who were with me in the ships at Mylae!" (*WL*, p. 62).

As a spectator, Tiresias empathizes, like the Lama in *Kim*, with the sufferings of his fellow beings bound on the wheel. As Christmas Humphreys puts it in his book on *Buddhism*, he is one of the few "whose lives are sufficiently unhappy, or who have sufficiently withdrawn themselves from the appearance of happiness in their own or in their neighbours' lives to be able to hear, in the stillness of the night or above the turmoil of the day, the ceaseless cry of anguish which rises from a blindly groping, sorrow-laden world."[18] Consequently, he is sensitive to the sufferings of those who inhabit the unreal cities of the world:

> What is that sound high in the air
> Murmur of maternal lamentation
> Who are those hooded hordes swarming
> Over endless plains, stumbling in cracked earth
> Ringed by the flat horizon only . . . (*WL*, p. 73)

This "ceaseless cry of anguish" mingles with the falling towers of the unreal cities to evoke a nightmarish vision of civilizations in chaos.

Tiresias thus bears witness to the fact of world-appearance or *māyā*. Because he has refined his consciousness, he is aware of his bondage to the wheel. He has only a hint of liberation—a tantalizing glimpse into "the heart of light" he once had in the hyacinth garden (*WL*, p. 62)—and only his "fragments" at the end—touchstones, to use Matthew Arnold's phrase, with which to test the stages of his inward progress towards the freedom of *nirvāna.* To encourage him on his way, he has the promise of grace—"a damp gust bringing rain" (*WL*, p. 74).

Unlike Tiresias, the speaker in *The Hollow Men* does not have the courage to accept his spiritual distress and to strive for the still centre of the turning world. Instead, he is sunk in apathy and thinks of himself as a scarecrow among other scarecrows, who shuffle despondently round the prickly pear or loiter beside "the tumid river" (*HM*, p. 85) like a throng awaiting the barge of Charon to ferry them to everlasting torment. He knows, however, that they are all in "death's *dream* kingdom" (*HM*, p. 84; my emphasis) and that they must remain "sightless" as long as they are content with their present existence. Moreover, he realizes that it is still possible for them to wake to reality and seek love through repentance. It is possible even for the hollow men to purge themselves of their desires, die to their self-centred existence, and storm "death's twilight kingdom" (*HM*, p. 85), where they might behold the "multifoliate rose" (*HM*, p. 85) betokening the ecstasy of the still point. But it is not easy, especially for those sunk in inertia, to cross "with direct eyes, to death's other Kingdom" (*HM*, p. 83). A "shadow" frustrates every feeble effort they make to transform their potential into the actual:

> Between the idea
> And the reality
> Between the motion
> And the act
> Falls the shadow. (*HM*, p. 85)

The shadow symbolizes the deceptive power of *māyā*. It is no child's play to wake up from the dream and penetrate the façade of appearances to the reality beyond. So, at the end, the hollow men continue to suffer in their cactus land and turn on the wheel, devoid even of the hope for grace.

The monologuist in *Ash Wednesday* is vouchsafed a light in the midst of darkness, a sign of grace amidst the delusions of *māyā*: he is blessed with a vision of "One who moves in the time between sleep and waking, wearing/ White light folded, sheathed about her, folded" (*AW*, p. 94). She is dressed "in white and blue, in Mary's colour" (*AW*, p. 94), heralding that which is beyond all shifting appearances and desires, and conveying to the protagonist's soul the possibility of the fusion of the human and the divine. Despite her silent affirmation of the Word, however, the protagonist is plunged into despair, for he is still in "the time of tension between dying and birth" (*AW*, p. 98), subject to the conflict between the values of the flesh and the spirit.[19] He has renounced his desires for "this man's gift and that man's scope" (*AW*, p. 89); no longer does he "mourn/ The vanished power of the usual reign" (*AW*, p. 89); nor does he "hope to know again/ The infirm glory of the positive hour" (*AW*, p. 89). Moreover, he fully realizes the limitations of the phenomenal world:

> that time is always time
> And place is always and only place
> And what is actual is actual only for one time
> And only for one place. (*AW*, p. 89)

Above all, he yearns to transcend the "unstilled world" and be united with the "silent Word" (*AW*, p. 96). Nevertheless, the *memory* of his desires still plagues him and causes him to waver "between the profit and the loss/ In this brief transit where the dreams cross/ The dreamcrossed twilight between birth and dying" (*AW*, p. 98). Even his longing for human love and sensual beauty deflects him from his purpose, for, in the final analysis, such love and beauty belong to the "unstilled world" of appearances; they too are *māyā*, reinforcing the dualism of the flesh and the spirit and barring the way to the non-dual reality beyond. Consequently, the delightful pictures that flash before his mind's eye—"white sails . . . seaward flying/ Unbroken wings" (*AW*, p. 98)—only breed attachment and the joy he feels is that of a "lost heart" for the ephemeral:

> And the lost heart stiffens and rejoices
> In the lost lilac and the lost sea voices
> And the weak spirit quickens to rebel
> For the bent golden-rod and the lost sea smell. (*AW*, p. 98)

It is all a delusion of "the blind eye" creating "empty forms"—the phantasmagoria of the turning world. Not surprisingly, the protagonist is baffled by the unreality of the forms, the insubstantiality of art as well as memory. He is caught in "the time of tension between dying and birth," wandering, one might say with Arnold, "between two worlds, one dead/ The other powerless to be born."[20] He is in a "place of solitude" where sexual, artistic, and spiritual ideals are all "dreams," and at a time when the symbolic gates to eternity formed by blue rocks and yew trees remain shut, awaiting the resolution of his inner conflict between the world and the Word. Like the soul in "Animula," he seems powerless to "fare forward or retreat" (A, p. 107). But, from the depths of his dejection, he miraculously finds strength to pray to the lady of his vision for deliverance:

> Blessed sister, holy mother, spirit of the fountain,
>   spirit of the garden,
> Suffer us not to mock ourselves with falsehood
> Teach us to care and not to care
> Teach us to sit still. (*AW*, p. 98)

In other words, he seeks a compassionate yet detached attitude (caring for others and not caring for the self), an attitude closely associated with the Buddha, who is invariably represented in painting and sculpture as 'sitting still' in the benign lotus posture of meditation. Only a serene and compassionate detachment akin to that of the Buddha, a humble acceptance of the divine will similar to that of the Christ, can enable him to penetrate the "falsehood" of "empty forms"—the illusions which "the blind eye creates"—and go beyond the "unstilled world" to "the centre of the silent Word" (*AW*, p. 96). Until that detachment and self-surrender are attained, he is under the sway of *māyā*.

Except for *Four Quartets*, all the major poems of Eliot—from "Prufrock" to *Ash Wednesday*—focus on the finite human consciousness and its gropings in "a wilderness of mirrors" (G, p. 38). These gropings and the accompanying thoughts and feelings all fall, in each poem, within the protagonist's own circle—a circle, we might say with Bradley, "closed on the outside" (*WL*, p. 80), constituting a private world of appearances. None of the protagonists in these poems succeeds completely in breaking out of the closed self and apprehending the reality that is. At best, some are vouchsafed tantalizing glimpses of the peace this reality entails; they can only be patient, endure, and await grace in their "unstilled world" (*AW*, p. 96). In *Four Quartets*, however, we sense for the first time that the poetic self has achieved at least a partial breakthrough. What has so far been obliquely alluded to as "the heart of the light" (*WL*, p. 62) or the "multifoliate rose" (*HM*, p. 85) or "the centre of the silent Word" (*AW*, p. 96) is now precisely defined as "the still point of the turning world" (BN, p. 173). Moreover, the peace and freedom that ensue when the human soul reaches "the still point" is dwelt on in the paradoxical language of the mystics. Of course, "the turning world" is still very much with us; it has not disappeared from the *Quartets*. But the apprehension of the still point, partial though it may be, seems to have subtly altered the poetic perspective, so that what goes on in the world is viewed not only within the boundaries of time, but also in the light of eternity. The creative word of the poet, like the all-engendering Word of the universe, brings order out of chaos. Consequently, the poet's efforts to find the word and the Word often appear identical mirror images of each other. Nevertheless, the poet's creative efforts ultimately take place in the temporal world of appearances; hence, they are subject to change:

> Words strain,
> Crack and sometimes break, under the burden,
> Under the tension, slip, slide, perish,
> Decay with imprecision, will not stay in place,
> Will not stay still. (BN, p. 175)

Moreover, the "shrieking voices" of unreason and chaos assail his words, forcing them to change continuously. Then, in a daring leap of thought from the temporal to the eternal, he shifts from "word" to "Word":

> The Word in the desert
> Is most attacked by voices of temptation,
> The crying shadow in the funeral dance,
> The loud lament of the disconsolate chimera. (BN, p. 175)

The Word is Logos, the complete meaning, the one reality that is, permanent and unchanging. When the Word becomes flesh, however, as in a Christ or a Buddha, it too is subject to the power of *māyā* and is assailed by "voices to temptation," phantasma, and death. The Word has to struggle against "the disconsolate chimera," enacting the same conflict that besets the soul of the protagonist in *Ash Wednesday*. Yet, in the eternal perspective, there is only the Word.

Clearly, all human attempts to describe either the still point or the turning world completely involve "the intolerable wrestle with words and meanings" (EC, p. 179), since they all take place in the realm of *māyā*. Also, knowledge derived from past experience has little value, for the "knowledge imposes a pattern and falsifies" (EC, p. 179). We are all groping, therefore, in Dante's "dark wood" or on the edge of the "grimpen" mire similar to that in Conan Doyle's *The Hound of the Baskervilles*, "where is no secure foothold/ And menaced by monsters, fancy lights,/ Risking enchantment" (EC, p. 179). In other words, we are all entangled in the web of *māyā*. This is obvious to anyone who has even momentarily apprehended the still point and is thus able to view his fellow beings and their actions in the light of eternity:

> O dark dark dark. They all go into the dark,
> The vacant interstellar spaces, the vacant into the vacant,
> The captains, merchant bankers, eminent men of letters,
> The generous patrons of art, the statesmen and the rulers,
> Distinguished civil servants, chairmen of many committees,
> Industrial lords and petty contractors, all go into the dark.
> . . . .
> And we all go with them, into the silent funeral.
> Nobody's funeral, for there is no one to bury. (EC, p. 180)

Since most humans cannot bear very much reality, they continue to dwell in ignorance, deluded by appearances and bound to the wheel, subject to change and suffering. Although there is but one Centre, most people live in centres of their own. This darkness of *māyā*, however, is not real; it may be vanquished by "the darkness of God":

> As, in a theatre,
> The lights are extinguished, for the scene to be changed
> With a hollow rumble of wings, with a movement of darkness on darkness,
> And we know that the hills and the trees, the distant panorama
> And the bold imposing façade are all being rolled away— (EC, p. 180)

The "bold imposing façade" of *māyā* vanishes,[21] and there is no more diversity; there is only the unity of *Brahman*, the one eternal unchanging reality. The still point has absorbed the turning world.[22]

In an essay on John Marston, Eliot tried to isolate a quality that sets poetic drama apart from prosaic drama, a quality discernible in his own plays:

> It is possible that what distinguishes poetic drama from prosaic drama is a kind of doubleness in action, as if it took place on two planes at once. . . . In poetic drama a certain apparent irrelevance may be the symptom of this doubleness; or the drama has an underpattern . . . the characters . . . are living at once on the plane that we know and on some other plane of reality.[23]

The characters in Eliot's plays may not always live on two planes at once; but usually they contribute to a certain doubleness in action. On the surface, they seem to take part in simple, realistic events; actually, they are involved in mythic or ritualistic acts. Either by deliberate symbolic *motifs* or by archetypal situations, Eliot conveys through his plays what he defines in his essay as "a pattern behind the pattern into which the characters deliberately involve themselves; the kind of pattern which we perceive in our own lives only at rare moments of inattention and detachment, drowning in sunlight."[24] Only gradually do we become aware of this subtly wrought "pattern behind the pattern," as if in apprehending it, we are re-enacting the poet's own painfully won apprehension of that greater pattern in which all contraries are reconciled. We become conscious of our dual citizenship in time and eternity and of a synthesizing power which acts through us and makes sense of seemingly opposite worlds.

The characters in *Murder in the Cathedral* have different powers of penetration: the murderous Knights, the Chorus of the Women of Canterbury, the Priests, and Becket have distinct conceptions of reality, ranging from the depraved worldliness of the Knights to the deep spirituality of Becket. The characters perform their different functions simultaneously: the Knights sin, the Chorus and the Priests suffer, Becket martyrs himself. This is 'tragedy' under the aspect of eternity, as it may appear to God: the arrogant self-absorption of the Knights, the uncertainty of the Chorus and the Priests, the soul-searching of Becket are all microcosmic. Becket intuitively grasps that the still wheel, as God beholds it, incorporates all the interlocking patterns of action and suffering which most of mankind can only view as flux. He knows that he has to combat deceptive appearances on his way to reality: "End will be simple, sudden, God-given./ Meanwhile the substance of our first act/ Will be shadows, and the strife with shadows" (*MC*, p. 246). He is not deflected from his purpose by temptations involving worldly gain. It is only when he is tempted by his own deepest desire for martyrdom that he pauses, unsure of his course. The Fourth Tempter flings Becket's own words in his teeth, and all four tempters chant in unison about the unreality (or *māyā*) of temporal existence:

> Man's life is a cheat and a disappointment;
> All things are unreal,
> Unreal or disappointing;
> The Catherine wheel, the pantomime cat,
> The prizes given at the children's party,
> The prize awarded for the English Essay,
> The scholar's degree, the statesman's decoration.
> All things become less real, man passes
> From unreality to unreality. (*MC*, p. 256)

Becket realizes with a shock that he is courting disaster by trying to impose his own will on God's and initiating action and suffering in himself and others, as if he, not God, were the centre of the wheel. The only way he can reach the still point is to surrender to the divine will. Those who act on their own initiative are inescapably on the wheel, but those who consent to the will of God are one with Him at the still point. Becket resolves, therefore, to submit and find his peace, like Dante, in God's will. His way through the miasma of *māyā* is now clear.

The Family Reunion too contains different orders of reality, corresponding to the potentials of the characters in the play. Amy, her sister, and their husbands are shallow, their vision circumscribed by the "normal" world of appearances. They see only events and cannot understand action that does not proceed from a selfish desire for sensory gratification. Harry reprimands them for their hollowness soon after his arrival:

> You are all people
> To whom nothing has happened, at most a continual impact
> Of external events. You have gone through life in sleep,
> Never woken to the nightmare. (*FR*, p. 293)

Harry is right in claiming that their life would be "unendurable" if they were "wide awake" (*FR*, p. 293), for they are people who have taken the reality of this world for granted, afraid to look beyond their ken. They are disturbed by Harry's passionate denunciation of their enslavement to the wheel, but they cling desperately to their world of make-believe:

> We all of us make the pretension
> To be the uncommon exception
> To the universal bondage.
>
> . . . .
>
> Why do we all behave as if the door might suddenly open,
>   the curtains be drawn,
> The cellar make some dreadful disclosure, the roof
>   disappear,
> And we should cease to be sure of what is real or unreal?
> Hold tight, hold tight, we must insist that the world is what
>   we have always taken it to be. (*FR*, pp. 301-2)

They are classic illustrations of the power of *māyā*, for they take the real for unreal and the unreal for real. On the other hand, Agatha and Mary see beyond appearances and help Harry to escape from "the universal bondage." When he comes back to Wishwood, he is in acute spiritual distress; he is dissatisfied with his life in the phenomenal world, but he has not yet gained access to the noumenal realm to which Agatha holds the key. Like the anguished protagonist of *Ash Wednesday*, he exists between sleeping and waking, in the "time of tension between dying and birth," and like him he is alone in his predicament. He speaks of

> The sudden solitude in a crowded desert
> In a thick smoke, many creatures moving
> Without direction, for no direction
> Leads anywhere but round and round in that vapour —
> Without purpose, and without principle of conduct
> In flickering intervals of light and darkness (*FR*, p. 294)

and yearns to escape being alone in "an over-crowded desert, jostled by ghosts." Later, he confesses to Mary his despair over his inability to escape his "shadows" (*FR*, p. 306). Harry's strife with shadows seems very real to him; nevertheless, as Mary points out, "it may be a deception" (*FR*, p. 307). Harry admits that what he sees may be a "dream." However, he is tormented by the thought that there is no other reality: "if there is nothing else/ The most real is what I fear" (*FR*, p. 308). Mary shows him that he brings his own "landscape" with him, one no more real than that in which his mother, aunts and uncles toil. She tries to make him see that contending with shadows is self-deceptive:

> Even if, as you say, Wishwood is a cheat,
> Your family a delusion — then it's all a delusion . . .
>   You deceive yourself
> Like the man convinced he is paralysed
> Or like the man who believes that he is blind
> While he still sees the sunlight. (*FR*, p. 309)

Harry is in the same position as a person who sees a coil of rope and deludes himself into believing that it is a snake. He is still subject to *māyā*. Gradually, Harry comes to realize the insubstantiality of the world of appearances and to question the reality of those around him:

> Nothing can have happened
> To either of my brothers. Nothing can happen —
> If Sergeant Winchell is real. But Denman saw him.
> But what if Denman saw him, and yet he was not real? (*FR*, p. 321)

Soon, he becomes aware of the change in his perception; he knows that this sets him apart from his relatives: "They don't understand what it is to be awake,/ To be living on several planes at once/ Though one cannot speak with several voices at once" (*FR*, p. 324). He can no longer speak their "language," for he has woken up from his sleep of ignorance and sees much more deeply than they do. He begins to discriminate between the real and the unreal and becomes detached from the transient phenomena in the normal world of appearances: "What you call the normal/ Is merely the unreal and the unimportant" (*FR*, p. 326). As his perception deepens, he realizes that *māyā* has entangled him in unreality:

>   Now I see
> I have been wounded in a war of phantoms,
> Not by human beings — they have no more power than I.
> The things I thought real were shadows, and the real
> Are what I thought were private shadows. (*FR*, p. 334)

No longer do the Furies, who have been hounding him, frighten him. They were a symptom of his inner darkness, causing him to see shadows where none really existed. As he emerges into the light of reality, the Furies are transformed into "the bright angels" whom he follows in pursuit of liberation from the "burning wheel" (*FR*, p. 339).

As we have seen, Edward and Lavinia, as well as Peter and Celia, in *The Cocktail Party*, are under the power of their private delusions and dwell amidst unrealities; they all come to realize this fact. Edward and Celia best express the helpless bewilderment and longing to escape which result when one is confined to a world of one's own making:

EDWARD: There was a door
          And I could not open it. I could not touch the handle.
          Why could I not walk out of my prison?
          What is hell? Hell is oneself,
          Hell is alone, the other figures in it
          Merely projections. (*CP*, p. 397)

CELIA: I don't hear any voices, I have no delusions—
          Except that the world I live in seems all a delusion!
          . . . .
          Then one is alone, and if one is alone
          Then lover and beloved are equally unreal
          And the dreamer is no more real than his dreams. (*CP*, p. 416)

Both Edward and Celia sense that "one is always alone" (*CP*, p. 397), and that one's thoughts and feelings all fall within "a circle closed on the outside" (*WL*, p. 80), constituting a private world of appearances. Edward, Lavinia, and Celia approach Sir Henry for relief from their suffering (presumably, Peter will follow in their footsteps). Sir Henry is quick to recognize their common *malaise*, but prescribes a different 'cure' for each. Obviously, they are in different stages of spiritual evolution. He advises Edward and Lavinia to accept the past and to perceive what they have in common—a sense of "isolation," which acts as a bond while they are still in "a state of unenlightenment" (*CP*, p. 410). They must make "the best of a bad job." Sir Henry has a much more radical remedy for Celia's sickness, for she is ready, like Becket, to sacrifice herself and accept martyrdom patiently and humbly. Sir Henry sends her to the "sanatorium" where only saints go, and Celia consents to "journey blind" towards the still point (*CP*, p. 418). Her life of self-abnegation "by which the human is/ Transhumanized" contrasts with the non-mystical life of average people like Edward and Lavinia. Celia's way is that of the contemplative mystic (the *sannyāsin*), who renounces all desires for the love of God; the other way, which Edward and Lavinia follow, is that of the dutiful householder (the *grihastha*), who consecrates all his actions to God. Both are ways of redemption, ways out of darkness through darkness, for "only through time is time conquered" (BN, p. 173). Sir Henry comments:

Each way means loneliness—and communion.
Both ways avoid the final desolation
Of solitude in the phantasmal world
Of imagination, shuffling memories and desires. (*CP*, p. 419)

Hence, Sir Henry's parting words to Edward, Lavinia, and Celia are the same: "Work out your salvation with diligence" (*CP*, pp. 411, 420). This death-bed exhortation of the Buddha to his disciples fits all those who strive to be free of *māyā*.

None of the characters in *The Confidential Clerk* is a martyr or a saint. None is an artistic genius; even Colby, who seems distinct from the others, has only a second-rate talent. None cures the ills of the mortal condition by recipe. The characters are all ordinary men and women who insist on their own diagnoses and make up their own prescriptions; yet, by the end, they all gain a measure of self-knowledge, though Colby attains the deepest insight. His self-education begins in the first serious conversation he has with his father. Initiated by Sir Claude's observation that his wife "has always lived in a world of make-believe," the talk soon strikes a profounder note, when Colby expresses his doubt of such a pretence: "It doesn't seem quite honest/ If we all have to live in a world of make-believe,/ Is that good for one?" (*CC*, p. 462). Sir Claude reveals to Colby that he had relinquished his youthful dreams of becoming a potter and gradually become reconciled to his substitute life as a businessman, which "begins as a kind of make-believe/ And the make-believing makes it real" (*CC*, p. 464). Nevertheless, he has continued to escape periodically into the world of his potter's creations. But it is obvious that the "pure" world of art into which Sir Claude escapes from time to time is as much a make-believe as the "sordid" world of business. He lives in "two worlds—each a kind of make-believe" (*CC*, p. 466). Like his wife, Sir Claude is a prey to "delusions" (*CC*, p. 462), caught in *māyā*. Colby can empathize with his father, since he too has abandoned his artistic ideals. But he rebels against his father's fatalistic acceptance of life's terms in the fond hope that "make-believing makes it real" (*CC*, p. 464). He refuses to be content with less than the wholly real. He too has a "secret garden," an inner world into which he occasionally retires, but he cannot accept what his half-sister, Lucasta, tells him: "it's only the outer world that you've lost;/ You've still got your inner world—a world that's more real" (*CC*, p. 472). Colby wants a "garden" as real as the literal one in Joshua Park, from which Eggerson, his predecessor in Sir Claude's service, not only gains creative joy but also "marrows, or beetroots, or peas" for his wife. To a man of Colby's sensibility, no reality is acceptable that does not integrate the ideal or spiritual with the actual or practical. He knows that both his outer world and his secret garden are insubstantial:

> my garden's no less unreal to me
> Than the world outside it. If you have two lives
> Which have nothing whatever to do with each other—
> Well, they're both unreal. (*CC*, pp. 473-474)

Moreover, he is alone in his garden; he longs for God to walk in it, since "that would make the world outside it real" (*CC*, p. 474). Mere ecstasy, aesthetic or spiritual, is not enough for Colby; it must be expressed through practical action and, more important, it must be shared, with man or God. Clearly, Colby yearns to break out of the closed circle of his self, the private world of make-believe, and be free of *māyā*. In the end, he does take his first step in this direction by becoming a church organist.

In *The Cocktail Party*, after Sir Henry has appropriately guided his "patients" onto their respective paths, his confidante Julia comments:

> All we could do was to give them the chance.
> And now, when they are stripped naked to their souls
> And can choose, whether to put on their proper costumes
> Or huddle quickly into new disguises,
> They have, for the first time, somewhere to start from. (*CP*, p. 421)

Lord Claverton, in *The Elder Statesman*, is also given a chance by the sheer force of circumstances to reform his life. He seizes the opportunity and, though it entails considerable pain, strips himself naked to his soul before his daughter and her *fiancé* and chooses to put on the proper costume. To start with, he is a sick and lonely man who finds himself aging prematurely. On his retirement from public affairs, he finds himself "contemplating nothingness" (*ES*, p. 529). All that he has done in life does not seem to amount to much, and he is left with the "fear of emptiness" before him (*ES*, pp. 529-30). Then he is suddenly confronted by two persons from his past life who accuse him of having adversely affected their lives. Forced to come to terms with his past, he finally recognizes that they are "merely ghosts" who have always been with him, tormenting his conscience (*ES*, p. 569). With this recognition, he emerges from his "spectral existence" into something like "reality" (*ES*, p. 569). When he has exorcised the ghosts of his past, his visitors are reduced to mere human beings who can no longer harm him. He confesses to his daughter and her *fiancé* and receives a kind of absolution from her. He now dares to be "the man he really is." This marks the death of his unreal self, that which "pretends to be someone" (*ES*, p. 582). In other words, he has battled with the accusing phantoms of his shadow self and thus loosened the grip of *māyā* over his existence. In the end, he is "brushed by the wing of happiness" (*ES*, p. 581), a sign that he is well on his way to freedom.

The characters and episodes in Eliot's plays are no doubt different from each other. Yet, their focus is on the deceptiveness of man's temporal existence and the necessity of living in the light of eternity. Man, as a rule, dwells amidst appearances and deludes himself into taking the unreal for real and the real for unreal. Consequently, he is enslaved by shifting desires and becomes bound to the turning wheel, which involves him in endless suffering. The treachery of carnal hopes and desires which enmesh man ever more firmly in *māyā* is thus Eliot's great dramatic theme.

The majority of mankind are subject to *māyā*, except for those odd and infrequent moments when they have brief and tantalizing glimpses of the reality beyond appearances. A few intrepid souls do achieve a breakthrough and find repose in the still point. What are the stages in their quest? What is the nature of their experiences? By piecing together the scattered hints in Eliot's poetry and drama, we might arrive at certain tentative answers to these difficult questions.

4

THE STILL POINT

From the unreal lead me to the real,
From darkness lead me to light,
From death lead me to immortality.
                    Brihad-aranyaka Upanishad

We might compare time to a constantly revolving sphere; the half that was
always sinking would be the past, that which was always rising would be the
future; but the indivisible point at the top, where the tangent touches, would
be the extensionless present. As the tangent does not revolve with the
sphere, neither does the present, the point of contact with the object, the
form of which is time, with the subject, which has no form, because it does
not belong to the knowable, but is the condition of all that is knowable.
                    SCHOPENHAUER, *The World as Will and Idea*

"The deeper design," Eliot writes in his introduction to Djuna Barnes'
Nightwood, "may be that of human misery and bondage which is universal."[1]
But the sensitive and discriminating individual can still penetrate "the bold
imposing façade" (EC, p. 180) of *māyā*, liberate himself from the wheel of
saṁsāra, be free of craving, compulsive action and suffering, and find *shanti*
or peace that passes understanding.[2] That such a state exists in the midst of
universal suffering and that this resting place in the midst of flux can be
attained by the individual is the overwhelming paradox of the great religions
of the world.[3] Thus, Krishna asserts that "the man of pure vision without
pride or delusion, in liberty from the chain of attachment, with his soul ever
in his Inner Spirit, all selfish desires gone, and free from the two contraries of
pleasure and pain, goes to the abode of eternity."[4] And the Buddha speaks to
his disciples of *nirvāṇa* or freedom *tout court* from the universal bondage in
uncompromising terms:

Monks, there exists that condition wherein is neither earth nor water nor fire nor air; wherein is neither the sphere of infinite space nor of infinite consciousness nor of nothingness nor of neither consciousness-nor-unconsciousness; where there is neither this world nor a world beyond nor both together nor moon-and-sun. Thence, monks, I declare there is no coming to birth; thither is no going (from life); therein is no duration; thence is no falling; there is no arising. It is not something fixed, it moves not on, it is not based on anything. That indeed is the end of Ill.[5]

Christ, too, affirms that the individual can find refuge from the woes of the world in the eternal being of God.

The poems published before *The Waste Land* focus on the cyclic purposelessness of existence in the phenomenal world and there seems to be little or no hope of escape from the wheel. Even Gerontion, who is disenchanted with the "contrived corridors" of history (G, p. 38) and speaks of Christ, the tiger, and of the "word within a word" (G, p. 37), is incapable of striking out for the still centre. Only once is there the barest hint of yearning for a life beyond the senses, and even that emanates from a non-human entity; the personified street in the fourth poem of "Preludes," trampled by insistent feet and weary of its own transitory show of fingers, pipes, and eyes, is

> moved by fancies that are curled
> Around these images, and cling:
> The notion of some infinitely gentle
> Infinitely suffering thing. (P, p. 23)

A Buddha or a Christ seems about to materialize as the poem trembles on the brink of a profound compassion for all suffering beings. But this moment of self-transcendence is shortlived and is succeeded by cynical indifference.

Initially, *The Waste Land* seems to have a vaster canvas than its predecessors, and the scenes and actors depicted seem much more complex than any we have encountered so far. The earlier poems focus on particular situations which illustrate the general human predicament. Our attention is usually captured by one person—Prufrock, Sweeney, Grishkin, or Gerontion— who reflects facets of our own personalities. *The Waste Land*, on the other hand, multiplies "variety/ In a wilderness of mirrors" (G, p. 38). Our interest is claimed by a host of incidents which take place simultaneously in the ancient and the modern world. Historical fact and literary fiction reside cheek by jowl. Characters coalesce and fuse, disintegrate and vanish, in a dreamlike manner with the nonchalance and unpredictability of the multitudinous gods of the Hindu pantheon; they are no one and everyone at once. The Waste Land, in fact, has no specific location in space and time; it harbours all beings of all worlds in all ages, who labour under the "universal bondage" (*FR*, p. 301) and long, even though only for a moment, to be free.

Tiresias experiences such a moment of freedom, which he cannot find words to describe, in the hyacinth garden:

> I could not
> Speak, and my eyes failed, I was neither
> Living nor dead, and I knew nothing,
> Looking into the heart of light, the silence. (*WL*, p. 40)

He has a momentary glimpse of the supreme truth, at once in and out of time. The hyacinth girl is a catalyst stimulating a harmonious reaction between the narrator and his environment, so that he gains a sudden insight into the centrality of being, where the spokes of the turning wheel converge. When he tries to recapture the experience in words, however, he is quite unequal to the task; he can only indicate it negatively: he could *not* speak or see, he was *neither* living *nor* dead and he knew *nothing*; yet, he apprehends "the heart of light, the silence." The negative and paradoxical mode of expressing the nature of *nirvāṇa* is quite common to both Vedanta and Buddhism. Thus, Yagnavalkya in the *Brihad-aranyaka Upanishad* states:

> That of which they say that it is above the heavens, beneath the earth, embracing heaven and earth, past, present and future, that is woven, warp and woof, in the ether. . . . It is *neither* coarse *nor* fine, *neither* short *nor* long, *neither* red (like fire) *nor* fluid (like water); it is *without* shadow, *without* darkness, *without* air, *without* ether, *without* attachment, *without* taste, *without* smell. (my emphasis)[6]

The Buddha refuses to limit the nature of freedom by defining it too precisely:

> There is, monks, an *un*born, *not* become, *not* made, *un*compounded, and were it not, monks, for this *un*born, *not* become, *not* made, *un*compounded, no escape could be shown here for what is born, has become, is made, is compounded. But because there is, monks, an *un*born, *not* become, *not* made, *un*compounded, therefore an escape can be shown for what is born, has become, is made, is compounded. (my emphasis)[7]

The Lama in *Kim* finds on attaining enlightenment that he cannot pinpoint the experience: "Then my Soul was all alone, and I saw *nothing*, for I was all things, having reached the Great Soul. And I meditated a thousand thousand years, *passionless*, well aware of the Causes of all Things" (my emphasis).[8] Perhaps the best explanation of this negative and paradoxical mode of expressing the nature of *nirvāṇa* is found in Schopenhauer's *The World as Will and Idea*: "the conception of nothing is essentially relative, and always refers to a definite something which it negatives . . . . Every nothing is thought of as such only in relation to something, and presupposes this relation, and thus also this something."[9] Eliot was well aware of the "subtleties" of the Indian philosophers,[10] directly from his reading of Sanskrit philosophy and literature and indirectly through Western authors such as Kipling, Edwin Arnold, and Schopenhauer. Not surprisingly, therefore, he adapted the oriental attitude in his own poetic evocation of enlightenment.

The momentary experience of enlightenment is pondered and cherished, amplified and enriched, to be savoured again and again in Eliot's poetry. Towards the end of *The Waste Land*, it is recalled vividly by Tiresias as a surrender of the individual self or ego to the overwhelming reality of the noumenon: "The awful daring of a moment's surrender/ Which an age of prudence can never retract/ By this, and this only, we have existed" (*WL*, p. 74). It cannot be found in "obituaries" or "memories," or "under seals" because it is not limited by space, time, and causation; the experience is indefinable, known only by its fruits in our daily lives.

The central paradox of *The Waste Land*, then, is that man, who is enchained to the wheel in the domain of *māyā*, can still emancipate himself from constant becoming and be one with the eternal being. Man is intimately related, in other words, to both time and eternity. This is why *The Waste Land* is full of references to both temporal and eternal values: we see the London crowds flowing down King William Street to "where Saint Mary Woolnoth kept the hours/ With a dead sound on the final stroke of nine" (*WL*, p. 62); we hear the gossipy Cockney women being asked by the pub owner to "HURRY UP PLEASE ITS TIME" (*WL*, p. 66)—time for what? to leave the pub? or to prepare for eternity by working out their salvation with diligence? —and we listen to Tiresias' ghastly parody of Marvell: "But at my back from time to time I hear/ The sound of horns and motors, which shall bring/ Sweeney to Mrs. Porter in the spring" (*WL*, p. 67). But man's relationship to time and eternity is not understood by most of us. Like the apostles on the way to Emmaus, we may not even be conscious of the nearness of Christ. Consequently, we lead a harrowing, anxiety-filled existence most of our lives:

> 'What shall I do now? What shall I do?
> 'I shall rush out as I am, and walk the street
> 'With my hair down, so. What shall we do tomorrow?
> 'What shall we ever do?' (*WL*, p. 65)

This bleak, horrifying, time-conditioned existence is, however, not quite hopeless; for it is possible for us to refine our consciousness like Tiresias and grasp how our time on earth may not just be endured or diverted but actively embodied and possessed, so that, however alone and unbelonging our 'I' may be, it can still break through, break *in*, and find something like the Kingdom of Heaven waiting there.

The apprehension of the moment of peace occurs suddenly in the hyacinth garden; later, it is spoken of as self-surrender. It is, therefore, a gift; in Christian terms, it is grace. Yet, individual effort is necessary to draw near to this moment; the entire action of the poem is *seen* and pondered by the blind Tiresias, so that his consciousness is gradually purified. He comes to understand that it is craving (*tanhā*) for evanescent things that binds him to the phenomenal world and makes him suffer.

The practical means of rooting out craving and eliminating suffering are drawn from the *Brihad-aranyaka Upanishad*: *datta, dayadhvam,* and *damyata* (*WL*, p. 74). Literally translated, these words counsel us to give, sympathize, and control; they also imply that we should practise self-surrender, compassion and self-control. Only by giving up the ego may we hope to attain *nirvāna* and fruitfully serve our fellow beings. Only by broadening our sympathy into a universal compassion for our fellow creatures imprisoned again and again in their earthly lives can we grow in awareness. Only by controlling our present lives, like an expert sailor at sea, can we "at least set [our] lands in order" (*WL*, p. 74). These lessons, imparted by the crashing chords of thunder, lend an optimistic note to the "fragments" which Tiresias, seeker of reality, shores up against the ruins of former lives. The poem concludes, therefore, by reiterating the instructions received from the thunder and intoning the formal ending of the Upanishads: Shanti Shanti Shanti (*WL*, p. 75)—a fitting reminder that, ultimately, the peace that passes understanding will prevail.

Taken as a whole, *The Waste Land* traces the journey of the human soul across the desert of ignorance, full of thirst (*tanhā*) and suffering (*dukkha*), to a vantage point from where the freedom of *nirvāna* is tantalizingly glimpsed, if not fully realized. Thus, the pervasive images of sterility and futility serve to stress the dark night of the soul in its emptiness caused by separation from God, while the positive moments point to detachment from craving as a means to emancipation. All opposites and contraries are reconciled in the exquisite moment in the hyacinth garden, the memory of which enables the seeker to survive. There are oblique references to the blissful experience of freedom from the universal bondage in the poems Eliot wrote between *The Waste Land* and *Four Quartets*.

The empty effigies in *The Hollow Men* are immobilized by despair; subject to selfish desires and deluded by appearances, they not only do not apprehend reality but also avoid working towards it. Their evasiveness is underscored by the image of the "eyes" they "dare not meet in dreams" (*HM*, p. 83). It is not clear whose eyes these are, but they challenge the human spirit; hence, the refusal of the hollow men to meet them indicates their spiritual bankruptcy. The fact that the hollow men shrink from "that final meeting/ In the twilight kingdom" (*HM*, p. 84) suggests that the eyes may be those of a saviour like Christ. Ironically, these eyes are the hollow men's only hope of release from suffering. Unless the eyes reappear "As the perpetual star/ Multifoliate rose/ Of death's twilight kingdom" (*HM*, p. 85), the hollow men are doomed to remain "sightless," bereft of any hope of salvation. "The perpetual star" seems to be associated with the Star of Bethlehem, which led the Magi to the infant Christ, while the "multifoliate rose" seems to be linked with Dante's image of the saints in Paradise, clustered together like the petals of a white rose. When Dante steeps his eyes in the river of light and looks at the celestial rose, he sees the eyes of the myriad Christian saints reflecting the glory of God, so that the rose appears to be a vast shining circle. This is the image Eliot evokes, according to Audrey F. Cahill, when he equates the eyes, the star, and the rose.[11] Together they symbolize the reality of God, whose absence is keenly felt by the hollow men in their cactus land. Sunk in inertia, however, they decline to strive towards this reality.

The single rose is essentially "a symbol of completion, of consummate achievement and perfection," and figures prominently in Western mystical literature as an image of unity.[12] To Dante, the "white rose" represents the fulfillment of his quest for the eternal Being of God. The "multifoliate rose" as a symbol of the reality beyond appearances is the Western equivalent to "the thousand-petalled lotus" (*sahasrāra*) of Eastern mysticism.[13] Tantrism, an esoteric branch of yoga, symbolizes the spiritual current in man as a serpent coiled up at the base of the spinal cord (see Figure 1). When the yogi (one who seeks to yoke or unite himself with the divine essence) advances spiritually, the current gradually uncoils and rises upwards, enfranchising a series of lotuses or spiritual centres in the body. The powers and perceptions of the yogi increase as the current travels from centre to centre. When the current culminates in the *sahasrāra* or the thousand-petalled lotus in the brain or the crown of the head, the yogi attains enlightenment; he is one with the reality behind all appearances.[14] Has Eliot then attempted an East-West ideosynthesis of symbols? Has he fused Dante's "white rose" (*candida rosa*) and Tantrism's "thousand-petalled lotus" (*sahasrāra*) to create a particularly arresting symbol in the "multifoliate rose"? Quite probably, especially since he uses the oriental and occidental symbols of the ultimate reality simultaneously in "Burnt Norton" to indicate a momentary experience of enlightenment: *the lotus blooms in the rose garden.*

A SYMBOLIC REPRESENTATION OF THE KUNDALINI RISING
THROUGH THE DIFFERENT CENTRES IN THE SUSHUMNĀ
TO THE THOUSAND-PETALLED LOTUS IN THE BRAIN

Fig. 1: From *Vivekananda: The Yogas and Other Works* (New York: Ramakrishna-Vivekananda
Center, 1953), facing p. 595.

The protagonist of *Ash Wednesday* is caught in "the time of tension
between dying and birth," struggling to detach himself from the temptations
of the phenomenal world and to unite himself with the changeless reality of
the noumenon. He knows from the start what Tiresias does not learn until
the end of his reverie and what the hollow men never learn: only by giving up
his egotistic craving for evanescent things and cultivating the capacity "to
care and not to care" (*AW*, p. 98) can he attain the ultimate reality and be at
peace. Hence, he intuitively apprehends the apparent contradiction between
the phenomenal world and the noumenon, between appearance and reality:

Still is the unspoken word, the Word unheard,
The Word without a word, the Word within
The world and for the world;
And the light shone in darkness and
Against the Word the unstilled world still whirled
About the centre of the silent Word. (*AW*, p. 96)

The movement of the world seems to oppose the Word; the world does not heed the Word and crucifies the Word made flesh in the person of Christ. Paradoxically, the world cannot exist apart from the Word, for the Word is within "the world and for the world." In other words, the Word is central to all existence, a perception precisely expressed by the image of the "unstilled world" revolving around the "still" and "silent Word." Significantly, the protagonist of *Ash Wednesday* resembles Tiresias when he tries to convey his insight into the nature of reality. He too perceives that the Word shines as light amidst darkness. He too has recourse to a negative and paradoxical mode of expression: the Word is "*un*spoken" and "*un*heard," "still" and "silent"; yet, it is the hub of all activity.

The experience of a supratemporal reality, negatively implied in the reverie of *The Waste Land* and tersely indicated in the penitential soul-searching of *Ash Wednesday*, is central to *Four Quartets*. The intimations of time and eternity, which have so far been churning in a rather vague and uncertain manner in the poetic consciousness, now become crystal clear. The dynamic contrast that prevails between the temporal world of constant becoming and the eternal world of being is illustrated through striking imagery:

At the still point of the turning world. Neither flesh nor
    fleshless;
Neither from nor towards; at the still point, there the dance is,
But neither arrest nor movement. And do not call it fixity,
Where past and future are gathered. Neither movement from
    nor towards,
Neither ascent nor decline. Except for the point, the still
    point,
There would be no dance, and there is only the dance. (BN, p.173)

Eliot's negative and paradoxical mode of expressing the nature of timeless reality finds here its fullest flowering. This attitude is common to both Vedanta and Buddhism, and Eliot probably adapted it to suit his own needs. He has not added essentially to the Vedantic or the Buddhistic description of the ultimate enlightenment. But he *does* articulate in moving words the psychological aspects of an experience which the individual may attain through Patanjali's yoga or the Noble Eightfold Path of the Buddha or the Adoration of the Madonna—the experience of the still point:

> I can only say, there we have been: but I cannot say where.
> And I cannot say, how long, for that is to place it in time.
> The inner freedom from the practical desire,
> The release from action and suffering, release from the inner
> And outer compulsion, yet surrounded
> By a grace of sense, a white light still and moving,
> *Erhebung* without motion, concentration
> Without elimination, both a new world
> And the old made explicit, understood
> In the completion of its partial ecstasy,
> The resolution of its partial horror. (BN, p. 173)

This evocation illuminates at least three aspects of the experiential reality: the "still point" is a state of enlightenment to be attained in this life itself and not in some world beyond death—the Kingdom of Heaven is within and at hand; it is a condition that transcends the senses, spells freedom from desire, action, and suffering, and bestows peace that passes understanding; it is both momentary and unforgettable, temporal and eternal, in time and out of time—a present where past and future are gathered and opposites are reconciled. These three interconnected *motifs* are heard again and again in *Four Quartets*. That Eliot explores their oriental "subtleties" in such rich detail, without ever sacrificing his fundamental Christian framework, speaks volumes for his poetic power of reconciliation and amalgamation.

The central emphasis of Krishna and Buddha is that *nirvāṇa* can be achieved here and now, in this very life, through renunciation of all selfish craving and through compassionate service to one's fellow beings. Then the darkness of ignorance is destroyed, the veil of *māyā* is rent, and the timeless reality is realized in one's own being—a process described by Eliot with deep and intense feeling:

> I said to my soul, be still, and let the dark come upon you
> Which shall be the darkness of God . . .
> I said to my soul, be still, and wait without hope
> For hope would be hope for the wrong thing; wait without love
> For love would be love of the wrong thing; there is yet faith
> But the faith and the love and the hope are all in the waiting.
> Wait without thought, for you are not ready for thought:
> So the darkness shall be the light, and the stillness the
>   dancing. (EC, p. 150)

Victoria & Albert Museum.   Crown Copyright

Dancing Śiva (*Naṭarāja*).   Bronze.   Cōḷa.   *c.* 11th century

Fig. 2: From A.L. Basham, *The Wonder That Was India* (New York: Grove Press, Inc., 1959), facing p. 329.

"The darkness of God" which annihilates the darkness of individuality and ignorance is an arresting symbol. Krishna uses it in the *Gita* in speaking of the *Jñāni* or the Enlightened One: "In the dark night of all being awakes to Light the tranquil man. But what is day to other beings is night for the sage who sees."[15] The *Jñāni*, according to Krishna, may even regard *Brahman* or the ultimate reality as the great *māyāvin*, the Supreme Poet who conjures up the vast drama of the universe and yet remains unaffected by it as a mere witness, knowing that the scene, the audience, and the very act of seeing are all contained in his own Being. By extending this profound symbol, the universe may be regarded as *līla* or Divine Play, culminating in the Dance of Siva in Hindu metaphysics (see Figure 2): "The essential significance of Siva's dance is threefold: first, it is the image of his Rhythmic Play as the source of all movement within the Cosmos, which is represented by the Arch; secondly, the purpose of his Dance is to release the countless souls of men in the snare of Illusion; thirdly, the place of the Dance, Chidambaram, the Centre of the Universe, is in the Heart."[16] Siva represents the noumenon, the centrality of Being, which sustains the phenomenal world of constant Becoming. He is the still point, without which there would be no dance. When one has merged one's individuality with the divine essence and is at the still point, one attains a condition of timelessness and partakes of eternity. All warring opposites resolve themselves into a harmonious pattern, "and there is only the dance." In short, the ultimate reality of God alone exists within and without the individual; the still point and the dance are indistinguishable, for "the darkness shall be the light, and the stillness the dancing." The Dance of Siva is also mimed by the worshippers of Siva in ritual in order to liberate the individual soul from the shackles of *māyā* and to unite it with God. Such a union, presumably, is the end towards which the rustics in "East Coker" are unconsciously moving by dancing round and round their country bonfire. Not only does their "daunsinge" signify "matrimonie" (EC, p. 178); it also tells of the concord of men and women, who, by ordering their lives in obedience to natural rhythms, are in harmony with the entire universe. In fact, all human beings, including the poet, "must move in measure like a dancer" (LG, p. 195), must consciously participate in the dance of life, with a joyous abandon akin to that of the worshippers of Siva or the rustics in "East Coker" if they are to be at one with God.[17]

The limitations of language are obvious when it comes to describing either the "still point" or the "dance," since the condition they hint at belongs to the eternal realm, while the words employed belong to the temporal world:

> Words move, music moves
> Only in time; but that which is only living
> Can only die. Words, after speech, reach

Into the silence. . . . Words strain,
Crack and sometimes break, under the burden,
Under the tension, slip, slide, perish,
Decay with imprecision, will not stay still. (BN, p. 175)

The tension is both fundamental and profound, between time and eternity, the phenomena and the noumenon, the relative and the absolute. The central paradox is that man, who is enmeshed in *māyā*, can still emancipate himself from constant Becoming and be one with the eternal Being. Man has dual citizenship, therefore, in both time and eternity and is capable of apprehending a point of intersection of the timeless with time.

The opening of "Burnt Norton" testifies to Eliot's preoccupation with time and eternity. "East Coker" concludes with the admonition that we must not give up our "raid on the inarticulate" (EC, p. 182) and cease to explore our interior landscape: "We must be still and still moving/ Into another intensity/ For a further union, a deeper communion" (EC, p. 183). This deeper exploration and communion with reality amidst the flux of existence is the chief concern of "The Dry Salvages" and leads to the truth of incarnation, to the apprehension of the point of intersection of the timeless with time.

The opening section of "The Dry Salvages" begins with the river within us and ends with the sea all about us. Our psychical inheritance of racial experience, what Jung calls our 'collective unconscious,' is likened at the outset to the flow of water in a river; this river is, in turn, compared to a "strong brown god" (DS, p. 184). The double comparison looks forward to the third section, in which the godly teachings of Krishna, urging Arjuna to be strong in life's battle, are pondered. Krishna is an *avatar*, an incarnation of the timeless reality (*Brahman*) in the phenomenal world: he represents "the impossible union" (DS, p. 190) of the timeless with time. He is also a destroyer of illusions: he teaches Arjuna that *Brahman* is the reality in its universal aspect and that *Ātman* is the reality within ourselves (cf. Christ's words: "The Kingdom of God is within you"); that *Ātman* and *Brahman* are indissolubly united to constitute one indivisible reality; that this one indivisible reality appears to be many, manifesting itself in innumerable ways in the phenomenal world of time and circumstance; and that owing to this power of *māyā*, there is an apparent separation between *Ātman* and *Brahman*. Therefore, Krishna urges Arjuna to surrender to the indwelling Godhead and act without brooding over the fruits of action—to be an instrument, in other words, of the timeless reality. In "The Dry Salvages," the river of racial memory, the "strong brown god," mutely attests to the microcosmic reality within us (*Ātman*), which is indistinguishable from the macrocosmic reality of the universe (*Brahman*). But this perennial truth of the human race is often lost in the Waste Lands of our phenomenal world and even forgotten in our mechanized and soul-less urban civilization. Truth, however, cannot be destoyed; it destroys everything else by its mere presence, "watching and waiting" (DS, p. 190) through all seasons, from birth to death, to claim us for its own.

While the river testifying to the truth of $\bar{A}tman$ is within us, the tossing sea of the phenomenal world lies all around us in all its immeasurable flux of beauty and terror. It is an ocean of undiscovered truth inscrutable to human reason; we cannot perceive the truth of *Brahman* behind and beyond the everchanging façade of *māyā*. All we have are the "hints" of its manifestations tossed on the "beaches" of recorded history (DS, p. 190); we have to infer the truth by means of this flotsam cast on the shores of existence and expand our limited human reason into the realm of intuition to realize that we are inseparable from the elemental life-force. As Krishna puts it in the *Gita*, "the river flows into the sea to become one with the sea."[18]

Out of the mysterious depths of this sea swells a symphony of voices prophesying eternity and sweeping us on irresistibly to thunderous images of truth that flood our interior landscape of illusions, hints, and half-truths. Our individuality is no proof against the sea's elemental life-force: the egotistic "I" of the opening lines is drowned by the impersonal chorus of the sea to reappear only when the teachings of Krishna to Arjuna are pondered in the third section of "The Dry Salvages."

The medley of sea sounds modulates into the clang of the "bell" (DS, p. 191) which tolls death to all our inner anxieties and conflicts in the time-conditioned phenomenal world and ushers in eternity. The river merges with the sea as our human sense of time is transformed into the eternal— "time not our time" (DS, p. 191). The $\bar{A}tman$ is at one with *Brahman*.

Indeed, man's intimate association with both time and eternity, properly understood, constitutes the core of religion, is what binds us back to God. But to most of us, the understanding has not dawned; we are so caught up in our regrets about the past or in our worries about the future that we are never quite conscious of the innocence and promise of the present: "What might have been and what has been/ Point to one end, which is always present" (BN, p. 171). We look before and after and pine for what is not, as Shelley points out, quite unaware of the eternal presence of the blissful reality of God. Consequently, we drag out a maimed half-existence all our lives:

> Neither plentitude nor vacancy. Only a flicker
> Over the strained time-ridden faces
> Distracted from distraction by distraction
> Filled with fancies and empty of meaning
> Tumid apathy with no concentration
> Men and bits of paper, whirled by the cold wind

That blows before and after time,
Wind in and out of unwholesome lungs
Time before and time after. (BN, p. 173)

This bleak, horrifying, time-conditioned existence is, however, not quite bereft of hope. There *are* intense, isolated moments when we glimpse the eternal:

For most of us, there is only the unattended
Moment, the moment in and out of time,
The distraction fit, lost in a shaft of sunlight,
The wild thyme unseen, or the winter lightning
Or the waterfall, or music heard so deeply
That it is not heard at all, but you are the music
While the music lasts. (DS, p. 190)

At such deeply perceptive moments, music is heard with such intensity that there is no longer a separation between the person listening and the music listened to; there is no "I" opposed to "music," for subject and object have coalesced and there is simply music: "you are the music." Such intense moments of aesthetic rapture, when the egotistical self is so completely submerged in the object of contemplation that it no longer seems to exist, are the closest most of us ever get to liberation from the flux of time-bound existence.

Three such moments seem to be experienced by the poet himself and are eloquently described: in the rose garden, in the arbour where the rain beats, and in the draughty church at smokefall. Of the three, the moment in the rose garden seems to be most vividly remembered and is movingly evoked at the beginning of "Burnt Norton." Speculating on the nature of time, like St. Augustine in his *Confessions*, the poet is arrested by the memory of an earlier moment in his life which he had not fully explored:

Footfalls echo in the memory
Down the passage we did not take
Towards the door we never opened
Into the rose-garden. (BN, p. 171)

The sharpening recollection of what might have been urges him to investigate the possibilities of the present moment:

Other echoes
Inhabit the garden. Shall we follow?

Quick, said the bird, find them, find them,
Round the corner. Through the first gate,
Into our first world. (BN, p. 171)

Suddenly, he recalls the earlier experience with such intensity that it seems
to unfold before his mind's eye; the present and the past moments fuse into
each other; time stands still and he experiences a momentary rapture:

And the bird called, in response to
The unheard music hidden in the shrubbery
And the unseen eyebeam crossed, for the roses
Had the look of flowers that are looked at. (BN, p. 172)

In this blessed mood, the poet and the companions of his memory move "in
formal pattern" and make their way to the dry concrete pool in the garden,
now mysteriously filled with "water out of sunlight," and witness the miracu-
lous flowering of ecstasy in the midst of sterility: "And the lotos rose, quietly,
quietly,/ The surface glittered out of heart of light" (BN, p. 172). The lotus is
a peculiarly oriental symbol, associated with ultimate reality in Hindu-
Buddhist thought. *The Tantric Way*, an examination of esoteric yogic practices, throws further light on the significance of this symbol in plain language:

Potent as it is, in tantric art the lotus is a symbol of the unfolding of the
self and expanding consciousness, which cuts through psychic opacity
and ultimately raises the aspirant from the dark depths of ignorance to
the radiant heights of inner awakening. Just as lotus plants grow in the
"darkness of mud" and gradually blossom out on the surface of the
water, unsullied by the mud and water which nourished them, so the
inner self transcends and transforms itself beyond its corporeal limits
uncorrupted and untarnished by illusion and ignorance.[19]

In *The Tantric View of Life*, an account of the tantric practices extant in
Tibetan Buddhism, we read this interesting interpretation of the lotus
symbolism;

Since early times the lotus flower has been a symbol of creativity
producing the world of things from its fertile seeds, and of purity,
because water does not cling to its leaves. This symbol is used . . . in
describing the peak experience of Being which is in *this world*, but not
just this world . . . a blue or white lotus flower or jasmine flower can
enthrall a person with its lovely colour, its softness and fragrance. That it

can do so lies in the fact that it grows in the unclean ponds of villages and hamlets, but is not affected by their uncleanliness. The same holds good for the attitude of the yogi. Even if he thinks of the objects of the outer and inner world, by knowing the real, he is not affected by the mire of the objects and taking the lotus flower without its (surrounding) mire, he understands the absolutely real without its (deflecting) ideas.[20]

Eliot was probably aware of the profound significance of the lotus. Certainly he was conscious of its mystical implications since he uses the lotus in conjunction with the rose, a symbol of the ecstatic union of the human soul with God in Western mysticism.

It is also quite likely that Eliot knew something of Tantra. He speaks of entering the rose garden through "the first gate" (presumably there are other gates), of moving into the "box circle," and of looking down into the drained pool; the pool is mysteriously filled with "water out of sunlight," and the "lotos" blooms in the pool. Diagrammatically represented, this seems to be the plan of the rose garden:

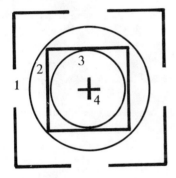

1. "the first gate"
2. "box-circle"
3. pool
4. "lotos"

In tantrism, the *maṇḍala*, "a composition of complex patterns and diverse iconographic images," is often used as an aid to meditation (see Figure 3). *The Tantric Way* gives a description of the structure of the *maṇḍala*:

> The predominant shape is the circle, or concentric circles, enclosing a square, which is sometimes divided into four triangles; this basic composition itself is contained within a square of four gates. Painted in fine brush-strokes between the spaces in hot reds, evanescent emeralds, soft terra-cottas and pearly whites, are labyrinthine designs, serene and static images of deities in meditative postures or terrific deities spewing out aureoles of smoke and flame ... all with symbolic meaning. The centre of the mandala projects the cosmic zone; it may be represented by a ring of lotus as the seat of the Vajrasattva, the embodiment of the supreme wisdom, immersed in union with his Sakti in a fathomless ocean of joy.[21]

A contemporary ground-plan of a temple based on a maṇḍala.

Fig. 3: From Ajit Mookherjee and Madhu Khanna, *The Tantric Way* (London: Thames and Hudson, 1977), p. 65.

Obviously, there are remarkable correspondences between Eliot's rose garden and a *maṇḍala*. The *maṇḍala*, moreover, is not a mere geometric pattern; it is full of psychic significance:

> The mandala indicates a focalization of wholeness and is analogous to the cosmos. As a synergic form it reflects the cosmogenic process, the cycles of elements, and harmoniously integrates within itself the opposites, the earthly and the ethereal, the kinetic and the static. *The circle also functions as the nuclear motif of the self, a vehicle for centering awareness, disciplining concentration and arousing a state conducive to mystic exaltation . . . .* The mandala is a psychic complex which conditions the return of the psyche to its potent core. Hence *the initiation process is*

often referred to as a "march towards the centre" so that the adept can interiorize the mandala in its totality, counterbalance the opposing dimensions projected in its symbolism and finally be reabsorbed in the cosmic space represented symbolically in the inner circle. The process of interiorization is a matter of orderly progression, wherein each inner circuit marks a phase in spiritual ascent . . . To evoke the universe of the mandala with its wide-ranging symbology accurately, the artist has to practise visual formulation . . . *The image, like a mirror, reflects the inner self which ultimately leads to enlightenment and deliverance.* In Tibet, the actualization of this awareness is known as "liberation through sight." The act of seeing, which is analogous to contemplation, is in itself a liberating experience. (my emphasis)[22]

Is Eliot disciplining the artist in himself by evoking "the psychic complex" of the rose garden? His poetic self does move "in a formal pattern" (BN, p. 172) along with other unseen presences, enacting a " 'march towards the centre.' " This process of interiorization does lead to a momentary apprehension of reality, if not to a total emancipation from a time-bound existence, and enables the poet to reflect deeply on the nature of man's relationship to time and eternity, on birth and death, on suffering and action. In short, by an extension of the symbolism of the rose garden, *Four Quartets* as a whole may be seen to be a *maṇḍala*, leading the poet and his readers towards a progressively greater awareness of unity in diversity.

The appearance of the lotus, then, at the climax of the experience in the rose garden marks the transformation of earthly desire into divine love. The moment of ecstasy, however, is shortlived, and the poet is once again caught up in time, "the form of limitation/ Between unbeing and being" (BN, p. 175). Like St. Augustine, he is left with the thoughts of childhood and innocence; they are the tokens of his brief visit to the lost Eden of the race.

Such intense and isolated moments, with no before and after, are not the still point of the turning world; they are but "hints and guesses/ Hints followed by guesses; and the rest/ Is prayer, observance, discipline, thought and action" (DS, p. 190). This fivefold path probably reflects the Noble Eightfold path of the Buddha and is no guarantee to emancipation. Eliot is quick to point out that total emancipation from the wheel of *saṁsāra* is at best rare and infrequent:

>   to apprehend
> The point of intersection of the timeless
> With time, is an occupation for the saint—
> No occupation either, but something given
> And taken, in a lifetime's death in love,
> Ardour and selflessness and self-surrender. (DS, pp. 189-90)

From one point of view, then, the still point of peace is the paradoxical intersection (or the impossible union) of the timeless with time; to the Christian, it is represented by the Word made flesh in Christ. An apprehension of this point, therefore, can only be through divine grace, though grace has to be deserved first in a "lifetime's death in love,/Ardour and selflessness and self-surrender."

From another point of view, the still point is a condition of freedom from craving and suffering which can be attained through individual effort. This is the Buddhist outlook, from which the notion of grace and the idea of incarnation are both absent.

Vedanta favours the middle ground between Christianity and Buddhism. The Upanishads and the *Gita* both stress the necessity of individual effort for attaining *nirvāṇa*. They also admit the operation of divine grace in human existence. The *Gita*, moreover, affirms that the timeless Being does manifest itself from time to time in an Incarnation or *avatar*.

Eliot is strongly attracted to the notion of individual effort as a means to the ultimate enlightenment. At the same time, as a professed Anglo-Catholic, he is unwilling to give up the idea of divine intervention. Thus, he provides apparently contradictory directions, almost in the same breath: in the third section of "East Coker," he counsels us to wait without hope, love, or faith for the "darkness of God"; but, in the final section, he affirms that "We must be still and still moving/ Into another intensity/ For a further union, a deeper communion" (EC, p. 183). Eliot seems therefore to set human passivity and activity at odds. In Christian theology, a mysterious reconciliation is effected where the individual is considered really free only when he acts under grace. The *Gita*, too, is unequivocal in declaring that self-surrender and right action ultimately mean the same thing and unite us with the eternal. Nowhere in *Four Quartets* does Eliot explicitly reconcile divine grace and individual effort; instead, he leaves us free to effect our own imaginative reconciliation. Indeed, the poetic appeal of *Four Quartets* lies in this voiceless invitation to participate in the poetic process, while the poetic power of the *Four Quartets* resides in the apparently unresolved conflicts.

As a Christian, Eliot is convinced of the unique character of the Incarnation of Christ. Yet in "The Dry Salvages," after dealing with the Annunciation, he introduces ideas and even direct quotations from the *Gita* before discussing the phenomenon of Incarnation. Krishna in the *Gita* is an Incarnation of the infinite Being of God, but he is only one among many *avatars*. Thus, the Christian doctrine of the unique Incarnation and the Vedantic perception of repeated *avatars* seem contradictory. They are reconciled, however, by the power of Eliot's poetry, for both Krishna and Christ manifest the timeless in time and illustrate the "impossible union" of two irreconcilable spheres of existence:

> Here the past and future
> Are conquered, and reconciled,
> Where action were otherwise movement
> Of that which is only moved
> And has in it no source of movement. (DS, p. 190)

Significantly, Eliot refers only to "incarnation" in the last section of "The Dry Salvages" and not to *the* Incarnation. Krishna and Christ both seem included under the generic term. Elsewhere in his poetry, Eliot indicates that the Indian thought systems may be regarded as preparatory stages to the full Christian revelation, so that Krishna (and even the Buddha) may be said to foreshadow the coming of Christ.[23]

It is possible to reach the still point by a positive or a negative approach. Extreme asceticism that seeks to conquer time by deliberate severance of all worldly bonds is common to all religions, but it has often been discouraged as an extreme measure unfit for most human beings. Eliot regards it as an escape from the place of disaffection and not as a means to transcend time:

> Descend lower, descend only
> Into the world of perpetual solitude,
> World not world, but that which is not world,
> Internal darkness, deprivation
> And destitution of all property,
> Desiccation of the world of sense,
> Evacuation of the world of fancy,
> Inoperancy of the world of spirit;
> This is the one way, and the other
> Is the same, not in movement
> But abstention from movement. (BN, p. 174)

The negative way resembles emptiness to Eliot, and so his description of it is rather grim. Such total renunciation enables the individual to attain the steadfastness of a rock against the flux and suffering of the turning world so that he can intuit the still point.

Contrasted with extreme asceticism, there is the positive way of detached action, which Krishna outlines in the *Gita* and which Eliot reinforces in the third section of "The Dry Salvages":

> At the moment which is not of action or inaction
> You can receive this: "on whatever sphere of being
> The mind of man may be intent
> At the time of death"—this is the one action
> (And the time of death is every moment)
> Which shall fructify in the lives of others:
> And do not think of the fruit of action. (DS, p. 188)

These cryptic words clearly hint at a unique discipline of action through which an individual may attain freedom from bondage to the phenomenal world. This positive way of action without desire for the fruit called *nishkama karma yoga* is, in fact, the central concern of the *Gita*. *Karma*, as we have seen, means 'act,' 'work,' or 'deed,' and stands traditionally for an action which inevitably produces certain impressions in the actor and determines the future action. Since we usually act out of self-interest in order to attain some end or fruit, such egocentric acts bind us to other acts, either immediately or at some future moment; this implies a series of births, deaths, and rebirths for us, the actors. Our own *karma* thus creates our bondage to the world. In order to be free, we must redirect our self away from an egotistic involvement with the fruits of our action to a loving concentration on the Universal Spirit, which is at once immanent and transcendent, in time and out of time. We must turn away from our lower carnal self (composed of desires, passions, and attachments) to our higher spiritual Self, which is identical with the Universal Spirit. We must let our little egotistic self die, and at the moment of death we must will the transformation of our entire being into an instrument of God. We must practise self-surrender, in short, to realize the Self and be free. Hence, Krishna repeatedly adjures Arjuna in the *Gita* to perform his action without attachment to the fruit of his action. It may be difficult to act in a spirit of self-surrender and say, like Christ in the Garden of Gethsemane, "Not my will, O Lord, but thine be done," but such selfless action is certain to lead to the still point.

Since we are bound by our own past deeds (*karma*) to the phenomenal world, we do not have 'free will' over the empirical events in our lives. But our nature and range of action are not necessarily confined to the empirical world. We are capable of functioning on a spiritual plane too. By performing our deeds without desire for the fruits, we may rise above the *karma* that binds us to the world and be free. We have to renounce our ego or lower self and surrender to our higher Self, identical with the Universal Spirit. When we have thus anchored ourselves in the source and substance of all bliss, all other attractions and distractions cease to afflict us. We are the *karma yogins*, those who act with a tranquil mind, treating all things equally. If we continue to act in this spirit of self-surrender, we are eventually free from the chain of events and the weary round of births, deaths, and rebirths. We are, moreover, free from the pairs of opposites, such as pleasure and pain, free will and bondage, for our freedom is not just the opposite of bondage. Our freedom is not on the same plane of being as our bondage; our freedom is in the spiritual realm, while our bondage takes place in the empirical world. Hence, when we reach the still point, we attain *mukti* or freedom of the spirit, pure and simple.

On an empirical level, then, progress towards the freedom of the still point, expounded by Eliot and endorsed by the *Gita*, denies us any 'free will.' But, on a spiritual level, it does require us to make the right choice. Our accumulated *karma* is bound to have its effects, good and bad. Nevertheless, if we choose to act in a spirit of self-surrender, giving up the fruit of our action, we will be free of the good as well as the evil effects of our *karma* and attain *nirvāṇa*.

With the air of a master initiating his disciple into the mysteries of human behaviour, Eliot points out that three modes of existence can be perceived within the phenomenal world—self-centredness, self-negation, and selfless compassion—in the third section of "Little Gidding":

> There are three conditions which often look alike
> Yet differ completely, flourish in the same hedgerow:
> Attachment to self and to things and to persons, detachment
> From self and from things and from persons; and growing
>   between them, indifference
> Which resembles the others as death resembles life,
> Being between two lives—unflowering, between
> The live and the dead nettle. (LG, p. 195)

Eliot suggests that the life-negating indifference of asceticism lies between the living and the dead. It grows, but does not flower; it strives to create, but is impotent; it is a living death. Eliot does not favour it as a means to emancipation; rather, he advocates the positive way of detached action described in the *Gita*. The still point is better attained through detachment than insensibility. Also, freedom from the bondage of attachment does not mean the end of love; instead, it enables one to pass beyond carnal desire (*kama*) to universal love or compassion (*karuṇya*), similar to that of Krishna, the Buddha, or Christ.

Detachment from self, things, and persons seems synonymous with the Christian virtue of humility. It is the only wisdom we can hope to acquire, and it is endless. It means surrendering ourselves so completely to God that we become an instrument in His hands, "a symbol perfected in death," casting off all pretension to knowledge and possessions, content to be led according to His will:

> In order to arrive at what you do not know
>   You must go by a way which is the way of ignorance.
> In order to possess what you do not possess
>   You must go by way of dispossession.
> In order to arrive at what you are not
>   You must go through the way in which you are not.
> And what you do not know is the only thing you know

And what you own is what you do not own
And where you are is where you are not. (LG, p. 181)

We are again confronted with the language of paradox. The ultimate reality is non-dual unity, while any attempt to describe it or the higher mystical disciplines necessary to attain it takes place in the realm of duality; hence, the description is bound to involve paradox.

Taken as a whole, passionate concern with man's spiritual destiny characterizes *Four Quartets*. They are, perhaps, the most intensely religious of Eliot's poems since they assert "the primacy of the supernatural over the natural life" (LG, p. 195). They trace the journey of the human soul from the darkness of ignorance to the dawn of wisdom, when the still point is at least perceived, if not fully grasped. Thus, "Burnt Norton" and "East Coker" stress the dark night of the soul caused by separation from God, while "The Dry Salvages" advocates right action as a means to emancipation. All opposites and contraries are reconciled through the prayerful accents of "Little Gidding," where all the "contrived corridors" (G, p. 38) of history are seen as a pattern of timeless moments, and all our explorations as a way back to our starting point. When knowledge matures, it becomes wisdom (*jñānā*) and issues out in right action (*nishkama karma*), which is indistinguishable from selfless devotion to God (*bhakti*).

The peace of the still point is securely in Becket's grasp prior to his martyrdom. He indicates this condition of "complete simplicity" clearly (LG, p. 198) to his priests: "I have had a tremor of bliss, a wink of heaven, a whisper,/ And I would no longer be denied; all things/ Proceed to a joyful consummation" (*MC*, p. 272). To arrive at this condition, he has surrendered himself completely to God and become a mere instrument in His hands; he dwells on self-surrender in his sermon: "A martyr, a saint, is always made by the design of God . . . . A martyrdom is never a design of man; for the true martyr is he who has become the *instrument of God*, who has lost his will in the will of God, not lost but found it, for he has found freedom in submission to God" (*MC*, p. 261). Becket's words are strikingly similar to Krishna's in the *Gita* when he urges Arjuna to surrender himself to the divine will and act without thinking of the fruits of action. The words, "the instrument of God," in particular, are exact English equivalents of the Sanskrit words used by Krishna—"*Nimittamātram bhava savyasāçin*"— which translates as "Be thou the mere instrument, left-handed archer!"[24] Becket has "only to make perfect [his] will" (*MC*, p. 271). He is content to be led to whatever end is ordained by God:

It is not in time that my death shall be known;
It is out of time that my decision is taken
If you call that decision

To which my whole being gives entire consent.
I give my life
To the Law of God above the Law of Man. (*MC*, p. 274)

Fully aware that his deeds originate in eternity, he acts with detachment. Consequently, he becomes "a symbol perfected in death" (LG, p. 96). He is also aware of what his martyrdom will mean to his fellow beings. He calms the agitated chorus:

Peace, and be at peace with your thoughts and visions.
These things had to come to you and you to accept them,
This is your share of the eternal burden,
The perpetual glory. This is one moment,
But know that another
Shall pierce you with a sudden painful joy
When the figure of God's purpose is made complete. (*MC*, p. 271)

The quiet words extend beyond the women of Canterbury to all who toil in the phenomenal world but are vouchsafed occasional "hints" about the noumenon (DS, p. 190). Becket's words are more than an assurance; they are a benediction.

In *The Family Reunion*, Harry receives "hints" from Mary and Agatha about redemption from the bondage of the wheel when he has almost given way to despair. He greets Mary's benign words with joy:

You bring me news
Of a door that opens at the end of a corridor,
Sunlight and singing; when I had felt sure
That every corridor led only to another,
Or to a blank wall. (*FR*, p. 310)

What Mary intimates to Harry, more through her sympathetic attitude than her actual words, is a brief glimpse of the rose garden. This becomes clear a little later in the conversation between Harry and Agatha. Agatha uses the rose garden to represent the momentary freedom she has experienced from time to time:

I only looked through the little door
When the sun was shining on the rose-garden:
And heard in the distance tiny voices
And then a black raven flew over. (*FR*, pp. 334-35)

Harry responds eagerly and recapitulates his own "moment in and out of time," naturally resorting to the symbolism of the rose garden:

> I was not there, you were not there, only our phantoms
> And what did not happen is as true as what did happen
> O my dear, and you walked through the little door
> And I ran to meet you in the rose-garden. (*FR*, p. 335)

Obviously, the rose garden represents a world of intuitive experience. Both Harry and Agatha are conscious of being freed from the prison of their individual selves and of being pierced with "a sudden painful joy" (*MC*, p. 271). But their moment of freedom is shortlived, for neither is fully emancipated from the wheel. Still, they vividly recall the moment which enables them to continue to work out their salvation with diligence. Harry, particularly, perceives the apparitions pursuing him to be his "bright angels" and gains the strength to follow them in a spirit of self-surrender (*FR*, p. 339). He is now wholeheartedly engaged in the "pursuit of liberation" (*FR*, p. 331).

As a preparatory measure, he gives up his "attachment to self and to things and to persons" (*LG*, p. 195). He renounces the family ties as well as the material possessions of Wishwood and resolves to follow his "bright angels" to

> the worship in the desert, the thirst and deprivation,
> A stony sanctuary and a primitive altar,
> The heat of the sun and the icy vigil,
> A care over lives of humble people. (*FR*, p. 339)

Agatha comments penetratingly on his decision to embrace asceticism:

> Here the danger, here the death, here, not elsewhere;
> Elsewhere no doubt is agony, renunciation,
> But birth and life. Harry has *crossed the frontier*
> Beyond which safety and danger have a different meaning.
> And he cannot return. (*FR*, p. 342)

The symbol of crossing is frequently used in Vedanta as well as Buddhism to denote the transition from constant Becoming to eternal Being. Krishna declares to Arjuna in the *Gita*, from the eternal perspective of the supreme Being: "This is My divine *māyā*. . . which is hard to pass beyond. Those who resort to Me alone cross over this *māyā*."[25] There is a similar claim in *The Dhammapada*: "Go beyond the stream, Brahmin, go with all your soul: leave desires behind. When you have crossed the stream of *Samsara*, you will reach the land of *Nirvana*."[26] The Pali term *pāraṅgata*, meaning "one who has crossed over to the further shore," is sometimes applied to one who has attained Enlightenment.[27] The Buddha is often referred to as the *Tathāgata*, meaning "one who has arrived there."[28] In other words, the seeker of reality crosses over from *saṁsāra* (the phenomenal world of appearances) to *nirvāṇa* (the noumenon) to arrive at truth. This crossing is made in *this* life. Thus, when Agatha speaks of Harry as one who has "crossed the frontier" and "cannot return," she does not mean that he will die; rather, she implies that Harry has crossed the border separating the unreal from the real. He is on his way to Buddhahood or Enlightenment. When he arrives at the still point, everything will be transformed in the light of eternity; hence, he can no longer return to a time-conditioned perspective of the turning world.

Harry's renunciation of his ties and possessions parallels that of Prince Siddhartha before he becomes the Buddha. Even Harry's departure from Wishwood closely resembles the departure of the future Buddha from Kapilavastu. Harry's car and his servant, Downing, are modern counterparts of Siddhartha's horse, Kanthaka, and horse-keeper, Channa. Both the horse and the horsekeeper are retained by Siddhartha as long as he needs them on the night of his Great Retirement. Neither is necessary to him beyond a certain stage for no external aid is required for attaining *nirvāṇa*. Similarly, neither his car nor his servant is essential to Harry once he is well on his way to the still point. Downing, who is as faithful to Harry as Channa is to his master, instinctively senses that his services will not be long required:

I have a kind of feeling that his Lordship won't need me
Very long now . . .
I've no gift of language, but I'm sure of what I mean:
We most of us seem to live according to circumstance,
But with people like him, there's something inside them
That accounts for what happens to them. You get a feeling of it.
So I seem to know beforehand, when something's going to happen,
And it seems quite natural, being his Lordship.
And that's why I say now, I have a feeling
That he won't want me long, and won't want anybody. (*FR*, p. 346)

In a famous parable called "Crossing over by Raft," the Buddha drives home the importance of giving up even wholesome possessions after they have served their purpose; to cling to them would be as foolish as to carry on one's head a raft that has borne one across a stream.[29] Evidently, Harry's car and his servant are superfluous to him beyond a certain stage in his quest for liberation.

Harry, then, is cast in the mould of the Buddha. Yet his renunciation is not contradictory to the spirit of Christianity. Christ repeatedly urges those who come to him to *give up* all that they have and to *follow* him. Harry, it must be remembered, *follows* his "bright angels" after *giving up* his family ties and possessions. Is Eliot, then, advocating the Buddhist renunciation in a Christian form?

By the end of *The Cocktail Party*, Celia too has "crossed the frontier." When she approaches Sir Henry, she is acutely conscious of the unreality of her existence and craves "the inner freedom" of the still point. She confesses that she does not really know what she yearns for, though she admits that she has experienced certain ecstatic moments of freedom from desire:

> I have thought at moments that the ecstasy is real
> Although those who experience it may have no reality.
> For what happened is remembered like a dream
> In which one is exalted by intensity of loving
> In the spirit, a vibration of delight
> Without desire, for desire is fulfilled
> In the delight of loving. (*CP*, p. 417)

She compares her bemused condition to that of a child who "suddenly discovers he is only a child/ Lost in a forest, wanting to go home" (*CP*, p. 416).[30] She does have a "clue" in "Compassion," as Sir Henry points out, towards finding her way out of the forest; she has already learned "to care" for others. Compassion, as we have noted earlier, goes hand in hand with detachment. Presumably, Celia has yet to learn "not to care" for herself in the sanatorium to which she is sent by Sir Henry. The parting advice she receives from him—"Work out your salvation with diligence"—echoes the Buddha's words. Actually, she works out her salvation in the traditional Christian manner; she leads the life of a missionary in a remote outpost of civilization called Kinkanja and becomes a Christian martyr when she is crucified by natives.[31] Self-sacrifice is held in high regard in both Vedanta and Buddhism, but the concepts of mission and martyrdom are absent from Vedanta, which does not proselytize, and are never emphasized in Buddhism. A Vedantin or a Buddhist would not deliberately court physical suffering and death. Krishna discourages self-torture in the *Gita*: "But false austerity, for the sake of reputation, honour and reverence, is impure . . . When self-control is self-torture . . . then self-control is of darkness."[32] The Buddha does not countenance extreme austerities either; in fact, he himself gives them up as fruitless: "But the six years which the Great Being thus spent in austerities were like time spent endeavouring to tie the air into knots. And coming to the decision, 'these austerities are not the way to enlightenment,' he went begging through villages and market-towns for ordinary material food, and lived upon it."[33] After attaining *nirvāṇa*, he forges the famous "middle path" for his followers, which avoids the extremes of self-torture and self-indulgence by practising self-control. None of the Buddha's followers has to undergo physical suffering before attaining *nirvāṇa*, except for an elder named Moggallana, who is brutally murdered by dacoits. This death, everyone agrees, is unworthy of a great one who had attained *nirvāṇa*. The

Buddha explains that Moggallana's death, though unsuited to his present incarnation, is the fruit of his *karma* in past lives.[34] Eliot does not furnish any such explanation for Celia's horrible death. She has already perceived the impermanence and suffering of the phenomenal world and learned the meaning of compassion when she comes to Sir Henry; presumably she cultivates detachment in the sanatorium. Why then is she crucified? The manner of her death is, to say the least, incongruous with her spiritual development.

We are driven to conclude that Eliot's attempt to preach the Buddhist askesis in a Christian form has not quite succeeded in the case of Celia. Sir Henry applies the Buddha's words to Celia appropriately, but the manner in which she works out her salvation is dramatically unconvincing; we are not *shown* the reasons for her martyrdom.

Edward and Lavinia, too, are advised by Sir Henry to work out their salvation with diligence, and their decision to adopt the ordinary life of compromise seems dramatically more meaningful than Celia's; it is better worked out in the play. They too are on their way to the still point, but much more gradually and harmoniously than Celia. Sir Henry comments: "Both ways avoid the final desolation/ Of solitude in the phantasmal world/ Of imagination, shuffling memories and desires" (*CP*, p. 419). His words are applicable to renunciation as well as the discriminating pursuit of life in the world. In short, Celia chooses the life of an ascetic (*sannyāsin*) to work out her salvation, while Edward and Lavinia elect to remain husband and wife and lead the lives of householders (*grihasthas*); both ways ultimately lead to the still point.

Sir Henry's advice—"Work out your salvation with diligence"—echoes not merely the counsel of the *dying* Buddha, but also the *daily* counsel of the Buddha to his disciples:

> Then taking up his stand on the landing . . . he would exhort
> the congregation of the priests, saying—
> "O priests, diligently work out your salvation; . . ."
> At this point some would ask the Blessed One for exercises
> in meditation and the Blessed One would assign them exercises
> suited to their several characters.[35]

The Buddha's advice is addressed to his monks, not householders, and he assigns "exercises in meditation" to suit their characters. Sir Henry resembles the Buddha in so far as he uses his words and guides his clients according to their temperaments. In prescribing a 'cure' to the ascetically inclined Celia as well as to the more worldly Edward and Lavinia, however, he imitates Krishna who outlines different paths suited to monks as well as to householders in the *Gita*. According to pristine Buddhism, Edward and Lavinia cannot attain *nirvāṇa* as householders. Vedanta is much more liberal in recognizing that such householders can be emancipated by fulfilling their duties as a consecration to God. Sir Henry might adopt the august and compassionate manner of the Buddha and use his words, but in extending their meaning to include Edward and Lavinia, he partakes of the broad spirit of Krishna. His words are more Vedantic than Buddhist in their significance. Not surprisingly, he calls the life of such householders "a good life" (*CP*, p. 417) despite its contretemps, and he sanctions the way of the ascetic as well as the way of the householders as a means to salvation.

The relationship between Sir Henry and Edward resembles that between Krishna and Arjuna. Sir Henry singles out Edward for help and gives him most of his advice, so that Edward seems chosen, like Arjuna, to be led out of confusion. Ironically, it is Celia, not Edward, who attains salvation, just as in the *Mahabharatha*, it is Yudhistra, not Arjuna, who emancipates himself from the wheel. When Celia's martyrdom is discovered, Sir Henry admits that he had foreseen her death: "When I first met Miss Coplestone, in this room, I saw the image, standing behind her chair/ Of a Celia Coplestone whose face showed the astonishment/ Of the first five minutes after a violent death" (*CP*, p. 437). Celia, though still alive then, is already dead to Sir Henry. His clairvoyance is remarkably similar to that of Krishna, who reveals to Arjuna that his enemies, though living, are already slain.[36]

In *The Confidential Clerk*, Colby has no clear notion of the still point; nor does he consciously strive towards it as Becket, Harry, and Celia do. He is much more concerned with right action. His true vocation and adopted occupation are at odds; though a musician at heart, he is employed as a confidential clerk. He is troubled by the discrepancy between his inner and outer worlds and yearns to make both real. In his confusion and in his fierce internal debate about his course of action, he resembles Arjuna on the battlefield of Kurukshetra. Just as Arjuna is cajoled out of his confusion into positive action by Krishna, so Colby is led out of his confusion by Eggerson, who offers him the opportunity to work as a church organist. Finally, when Colby decides to be a musician, he acts essentially in accordance with the teaching of Krishna in the *Gita*: "And do thy duty, even if it be humble, rather than another's even if it be great. To die in one's duty is life; to live in another's is death."[37] Of course, Colby is not quite ready to act in a spirit of self-surrender, giving up the fruit of action; he is not enthusiastic about Eggerson's suggestion that he should make spiritual capital out of sacred music and eventually become a minister. Nevertheless, even his present determination to follow his true vocation is a step in the right direction, an attempt at right action that will bear fruit in his life as well as in others' lives and ultimately lead to the still point.

Though Colby is unaware of the still point, he has access to a "secret garden" to which he can retire and hear "a music that no one else could hear" (*CC*, p. 473). There he is vouchsafed certain oblique "hints" (DS, p. 190) about the ultimate reality, but he has not yet refined his awareness to actively strive towards it. All that he is conscious of is an awful feeling of being "alone"; he senses that if God would walk in his garden, he would no longer be alone and even the world outside would become "real" and "acceptable" (*CC*, p. 474). But God has not yet appeared; significantly, neither a rose nor a lotus blooms in Colby's garden.

There is no mention of either the still point or the rose garden in *The Elder Statesman*. However, Lord Claverton rejoices at the end of having been "*freed* from the self that pretends to be someone" (*ES*, p. 582; my emphasis), and when at last he dares to be "the man he really is," he speaks in a language reminiscent of Becket's when he becomes "an instrument of God":

> I feel at peace now
> It is the peace that ensues upon contrition
> When contrition ensues upon knowledge of the truth.
>
> . . . .
>
> I've only just now had the illumination
> Of knowing what love is. We all think we know,
> But how few of us do! And now I feel happy—
> In spite of everything, in defiance of reason,
> I have been brushed by the wing of happiness. (*ES*, p. 581)

Clearly, Lord Claverton is now aware of something beyond the daily round of his existence. His daughter, Monica, is quick to perceive his transformation and observes to her *fiancé*, Charles, that her father "has gone too far to return" to them (*ES*, p. 583). Like Harry, he has "crossed the frontier" (*FR*, p. 342), passed from the unreal to the real, and is on his way to the still point.

All the protagonists in Eliot's plays advance along the spokes of the wheel of *saṁsāra* towards the still point. The paths they pursue and the ideas they articulate vary according to their temperaments, but the end they have in view is the same, which is completely in accordance with what Krishna states in the *Gita*, speaking from the eternal perspective of God: "In any way that men love me in that same way they find my love; for many are the paths of men, but they all in the end come to me."[38] Other characters lack the clarity of vision which the protagonists eventually attain. Nevertheless, they become aware of the change in the protagonists and react to it; in this lies their salvation. "They have not seen the Father, but they have seen the Son, and they who have seen the Son have seen the Father also." Erring mortals they may be, full of deceit and treachery; still, they too are being drawn irresistibly and unknowingly towards the centre. The subsidiary characters revolve around the protagonists, while the protagonists revolve around the still point.

What we witness in Eliot's dramas is an 'acting out' of the philosophical themes he explores in his poetry, particularly in *Four Quartets*. What we perceive is "the pattern behind the pattern,"[39] unity in diversity. What we gain is the awareness that we, too, are part of the greater pattern, while our attention is centred on the actors who are all orbiting around the still point.

Eliot does not elaborate on the nature of the still point. Instead, he leaves us the task of piecing together the hints scattered throughout his poetry and drama, particularly *Four Quartets*, and of forming a coherent picture: the still point is thus "a liberation/ From the future as well as the past" (LG, p. 195); it does not, however, negate time, for when we are liberated, we consider "the future/ And the past with an equal mind" (DS, p. 188); in other words, past and future are reconciled in an eternal now. The still point spells "inner freedom from the practical desire" (BN, p. 173), but freedom from desire is not desirelessness, for there is still the "unattached devotion which might pass for devotionless" (DS, p. 186) and "the expanding of love beyond desire" (LG, p. 195). The still point is "release from the inner and outer compulsion"(BN, p. 173), but it is not inaction, for "right action is freedom/ From past and future also" (DS, p. 190), and we act freely when we have surrendered our will to the Source of all our strength, the noumenal reality within us.

The still point is thus not freedom from time and space, but freedom from the feeling of being confined by time and space; not freedom from desire, but freedom from the slavery to shifting desires; not freedom from suffering, but freedom from the crushing power of suffering, through understanding and compassion; not freedom from death—for "the time of death is every moment"(DS, p. 188)—but freedom from the fear of death.

When we reach the still point, then, we attain *mukti* or freedom *tout court*, a condition of "complete simplicity" (LG, p. 198). And as *jivan-muktas*, those who have attained freedom in this life itself, we live unattached and cling to nothing in the world, transcending, not denying, impermanence and suffering. Or, as Iqbal Singh expresses it eloquently in his book, *Gautama Buddha*:

> Here we are in a universe which is devoid of tension—not because contraries and conflicts have ceased to operate, but because they have somehow become intelligible. Here, in the very contemplation of transiency, we receive a measure of eternity . . . Here the wheel turns and does not turn. Here the paradox is no longer a paradox, but rather a luminous certitude. Here we are in the very heart of peace.[40]

CONCLUSION

The One Reality

Tat tvam asi, Svetaketu. Thou art THAT.
Chandogya Upanishad

The unreal never is; the real never is not.
The Bhagavad Gita

Our comparison of the fundamental perceptions underlying Eliot's poetry and drama with those of Vedanta and Buddhism has brought to light a number of correspondences between Eliot's poetic vision and Indian philosophical thought. These correspondences are too striking to be mere coincidence, too frequent to be fortuitous. Obviously, the "subtleties" of the Indian philosophers are significant to an understanding of Eliot's vision of the human condition.

It is clear that Eliot's philosophical and spiritual orientation is essentially in accordance with the basic tenets of Christianity as well as those of Vedanta and Buddhism and that these truths are fused together in his poetry and drama.[1] Consequently, there is, at first, the penetrating awareness of the pervasiveness of suffering and impermanence, the tragic awareness that "the deeper design is that of human misery and bondage which is universal."[2] Next, there is the recognition that the root-cause of all suffering is the craving that impels us to cling to transient material phenomena. Then, there is the realization that through the practice of detachment from egotistic craving and selfless compassion towards those who suffer, the universal change and suffering can be transcended, though not negated, in the apprehension of the timeless in time. Above all, there is the deep feeling that permeates Eliot's works from beginning to end, the heartfelt yearning for a mystic union with the Ultimate Reality in one's own being, a yearning born out of the conviction that one must work out one's salvation with diligence and expressed through passionate prayer which his poetry and drama may be said to embody in the last analysis.

The basic concern that animates Eliot's poetic "raids on the inarticulate" (EC, p. 182) — the awareness of the fact of human bondage in time and the possibility of human freedom in eternity — is absolutely universal and may well be called the *philosophia perennis* that surfaces variously time and again in the religious and philosophical traditions of the East and the West. Thus, the same awareness of human frailty and strength at the core of *The Waste Land* or *Four Quartets* is found in *The Bhagavad Gita*, the Buddha's Fire Sermon, and the Sermon on the Mount. A similar preoccupation with the timeless underlies the wisdom of Yagnavalkya in the *Brihad-aranyaka Upanishad* and the penitential soul-searching of St. Augustine in his *Confessions*, separated though they are by time and space. Herein lies our justification for reading Eliot's poetry in the light of the *Brihad-aranyaka Upanishad*, or the Fire Sermon, or even the New Testament; not only do they enable us to grasp the keen perceptions underlying his poetry, but they also impart an unearthly radiance to his vision that teases us into the realm of the eternal. In a lucid and penetrating essay called "The Minimum Working Hypothesis," Aldous Huxley has outlined the fundamental intuitions of the perennial philosophy:

> That there is a Godhead, Ground, Brahman, Clear Light of the Void, which is the unmanifested principle of the universe.
> That the Ground is at once transcendent and immanent.
> That it is possible for human beings to love, know and, from virtually, to become actually identical with the divine Ground.
> That to achieve this unitive knowledge of the Godhead is the final end and purpose of human existence.
> That there is a Law or Dharma which must be obeyed, a Tao or a Way which must be followed, if men are to achieve this final end.
> That the more there is of self, the less there is of the Godhead; and that the Tao is therefore a way of humility and love, the Dharma a living law of mortification and self-transcending awareness.[3]

Consequently, it is idle for us to claim that Eliot is refreshingly original in his insights.[4] What we can and must recognize, however, are his *clear understanding*, his *masterful blending*, and his *powerful sounding* of the *leitmotifs* of Vedantic, Buddhist, and Christian writings in his poetry and drama. These are the unique characteristics that set him apart from his contemporaries, many of whom turn to the ancient East or West for inspiration and guidance in an Age of Anxiety. Yeats, for instance, makes periodic inroads into Eastern and Western mysticism, but he is easily sidetracked from purely philosophical concerns to occult practices, so that the vision that emerges lacks clarity. Pound's spasmodic dabblings in Buddhism are unconvincing and shot through with error. Huxley's encyclopaedic knowledge is no doubt admirable, but he attempts a philosophical, not a poetic, synthesis. After making all valid discounts, Eliot's eclecticism is the most convincing and comprehensive in modern poetry. It is also remarkably free of all pretentiousness and sentimentality, of the misunderstanding born out of self-pity and of the vanity originating in self-glorification, which are the hallmarks of the romantic decadence — perhaps most clearly exemplified in the flamboyant figure of Oscar Wilde. Eliot's vision is also one of the most reliable, if we are looking for a momentary stay against confusion in the contemporary chaos.

It may be objected that Eliot's commitment to Christianity inhibits his vision, resulting in contradictions, where there need be none (for example, his rather unconvincing effort to reconcile the Christian Incarnation with the Hindu *avatar*). On the other hand, critics like Helen Gardner find it difficult to deal with Eliot's apparent idiosyncrasy in venturing far beyond the bounds of his Christianity. Though a professed Anglo-Catholic, he includes unorthodox and even non-Christian elements in his poetry and drama. Unable to understand this, the critics tend to slight the 'Indian aspect' of Eliot or even disapprove of Eliot's 'magpie' habit of accumulating 'tidbits' from various sources. Helen Gardner, for instance, finds the introduction of Krishna and the *Gita* in "The Dry Salvages" an error.[5]

From the strictly Christian point of view, Christ is *the* Incarnation, the only means of salvation for the individual. Eliot obviously accepts this. Why, then, does he incorporate *odd* ideas from other religions? A valid question, no doubt. But Eliot does not provide a clear-cut answer, leaving his poetry to speak for itself. Unfortunately, his critics take his silence to be a confession of failure, failure to reconcile apparently contradictory doctrines.

But to those familiar with Indian philosophy, there is really no contradiction. As we have pointed out, Hindu thought is basically flexible and liberal and permits varied doctrinal viewpoints within the fold of a single religion. Arthur Osborne writes with great perception:

> There are of course great differences of understanding between man and man, as in all religions, but the religion itself is the same. What distinguishes Hinduism from more uniform religions is merely its enormous scope, offering diverse levels of understanding and modes of approach .... If Truth stands solid, like a mountain, it may wear a different face as seen from every side and different paths may lead up to it, running at short range in different directions.[6]

According to the non-dualistic interpretation of the key texts of Hinduism, Truth or Absolute Reality is unknowable by human reason, so that all speculations and practices are merely 'minimum working hypotheses' for the attainment of this Reality. Consequently, the individual is free to pursue any path that suits his temperament and even borrow ideas or derive inspiration from other paths. Thus, when Eliot shows an inclination towards the teachings of Krishna or the Buddha, while retaining his strong bond to Christianity, there is no contradiction in his outlook from the Indian point of view. In Hindu terms, Christ too is an *avatar*, a Saviour, and an Incarnation of God, and to seek Truth or Absolute Reality through him is a perfectly valid procedure. Moreover, in the Hindu view of life, it is not necessary for the individual to be 'converted' to a different creed in order to seek Reality. In fact, Krishna positively discourages conversion in the *Gita*: "And do thy duty, even if it be humble, rather than another's, even if it be great. To die in one's duty is life: to live in another's is death."[7] "Duty" here has the wider connotation of one's natural bent of mind or *norm* in life. In the Hindu view of life, the search for the ultimate Reality takes precedence over the particular means an individual adopts in his search. To be one with the eternal Godhead: this is the unifying principle of Hindu thought which keeps all the alternate ways to Truth in purposeful togetherness.

This is where Eliot's eclectic temperament coincides with the all-embracing attitude of Hindu thought. As we have already remarked in the Introduction, Eliot is best thought of as a '*kavi*' or a poet-philosopher in the Indian sense of the term, as one who is more interested in seeking "the still point of the turning world" — a unifying principle of the universe that transcends the flux and suffering of the phenomenal world — through his poetry than in constructing a logical and systematic worldview. It is quite appropriate, therefore, that he should retain his fundamental Christian framework while incorporating Hindu-Buddhist ideas in his poetry and drama. This does not imply that Eliot is less a Christian poet than he is universally acknowledged to be; rather, this indicates that Eliot's poetic approach to "the still point" is remarkably similar to the tolerant and pragmatic approach of the "Forest Philosophers" who composed the Upanishads and of Krishna, the divine author and spokesman of the *Gita*.

Eliot's affinity to the Hindu view of life, particularly that which finds expression in the Upanishads and the *Gita*, is apparent despite his strong early attraction towards Buddhism. We know that Eliot was tremendously impressed by the noble and compassionate life of the Buddha. We know too that at the time of writing *The Waste Land* he contemplated becoming a Buddhist. And we have seen how he borrows Buddhist ideas and symbols (which have a great deal in common with Hindu ideas and symbols) and makes use of them in his poetry and drama.

A bird's-eye view of Eliot's works reveals that the austere spirit of Buddhism is most pronounced in *The Waste Land*. The poem evokes an atmosphere of intense spiritual distress and advocates a thoroughgoing renunciation of the life of the senses. By repeating a single word, "burning," which he borrows from the Buddha's Fire Sermon, Eliot forcefully underscores the central thought of the poem: we are all afire and burning with carnal desires, and we thirst for their gratification; consequently, our lives are full of suffering, and we spend most of our lives wandering in a spiritual waste land. Implicit in the poem is the counsel that we should renounce our thirst or craving for the transitory things of this world in order to be free of suffering. Apparently, Eliot is responding to the ascetic spirit of Buddhism, whose central teaching is that the freedom of *nirvāṇa* can be attained through self-denial. The severity of this Buddhist injunction is only partially tempered by Eliot's appeal to the crashing chords of thunder towards the end of the poem. The Upanishadic thunder counsels us to be charitable, compassionate, and self-controlled, but it does not wholly mitigate the cauterizing effect of the Buddhist counsel. We are left, therefore, with an overwhelming impression that this phenomenal world must be completely forsaken in order to gain the everlasting peace of *nirvāṇa*. In other words, the poem as a whole creates in us an aversion towards the life of the senses in this world.

But as we progress from *The Waste Land* (1922) towards *The Elder Statesman* (1959), we detect a gentle but remarkable change in Eliot's attitude. There is actually an unusual development from renunciation to an acceptance of life, from asceticism to tolerance. The strong aversion which Eliot shows as a young man towards the life of the senses is gradually toned down, though the superiority of the self-abnegating contemplative individual is always recognized. We first find Eliot accepting the life of the householder, as opposed to the life of the ascetic, as a 'good life' in *The Cocktail Party* (1950). Not surprisingly, therefore, his last two plays, *The Confidential Clerk* (1954) and *The Elder Statesman* (1959), are built around the close-knit structure of the family, sanctifying the life of the householder rather than that of the contemplative mystic.

Eliot seems to have definitely changed his perspective, therefore, from asceticism, so conspicuous in *The Waste Land*, to an acceptance of life and humanity in the world. In short, we see him gently drifting from Buddhism to Vedanta — towards the ideal preached by Krishna in the *Gita*, that of acting in a spirit of self-surrender, without caring for the fruit of action, regardless of the particular role we play in life. This shift in Eliot's attitude can be observed as early as the concluding section of *The Waste Land*, where he invokes the voice of the thunder of the Upanishads to temper the severity of the Buddha's Fire Sermon. The shift becomes more marked in "The Dry Salvages," where the figures of Krishna and Arjuna stand for the resolute pursuit of life, admonishing us that we must accept the consequences of our past deeds and die every moment to our egotistic selves in order that we may partake of eternity. The shift is definitely achieved in *The Cocktail Party*, where the Buddhist, Hindu, and even Christian ideas are perfectly synthesized.

The framework of the *Bhagavad Gita* seems to coincide with Eliot's mature worldview. Its all-embracing universality and tolerance seem particularly well-suited to Eliot's own mellowed philosophy of life. Indeed, with the exception of Dante's *Divine Comedy*, no work seems more relevant to an understanding of Eliot's poetry and drama than the *Bhagavad Gita*. Not only does it synthesize Buddhist and Hindu ideas and broaden them into an acceptance of humanity, it also harmonizes well with Eliot's particular form of Christianity.

The non-Christian elements in Eliot's poetry and drama are there with a definite purpose; they are not present owing to some odd fancy of an idiosyncratic poet. Eliot gradually assimilates them and establishes a natural and poetic reconciliation. He is certainly not following a process of elimination in order to reach the full Christian revelation. Instead, he is deliberately reaching out beyond the confines of his Anglo-Catholicism and Occidental personality in a genuine attempt at East-West ideosynthesis.

Above all, we must remember that Eliot is neither a dogmatic theologian, determined to propagate his creed, nor an academic philosopher, bent on expounding his system; he is a *kavi*, a poet who attempts to see deep into the design of the universe and to embody his intuitive responses in poetry and drama. Hence, the apparently unresolved conflicts and inexplicable paradoxes in his poetry and drama do not undermine his vision; instead, they add strength to it.

Ultimately, what gives Eliot's poetry and drama an enduring beauty and a penetrating power is the fact that he has perceived the perennial and most ancient truth of humanity and invoked THAT which is universal and eternal, common to both the East and the West.

In the end, of course, what matters is the vision and what we do about the vision. We must never mistake the sign for the thing signified and cease from our exploration for a condition of complete simplicity. We should try to make perfect our will like Thomas Becket and move towards the ageless enigma that resides in the inmost centre of our being. When our journey to the still point is an accomplished fact, then, and only then, shall the poet's prophecy become a reality:

> all shall be well
> All manner of thing shall be well
> When the tongues of flame are in-folded
> Into the crowned knot of fire
> And the fire and the rose are one. (LG, p. 198)

NOTES

NOTES TO THE INTRODUCTION

1. Montgomery Belgion, "Irving Babbitt and the Continent," in *T.S. Eliot: A Symposium for His Sixtieth Birthday* (N.Y.: Books for Libraries Press, 1968), p. 85.
2. E.F.C. Ludowyk, "T.S. Eliot in Ceylon," *T.S. Eliot: A Symposium*, p. 105.
3. Philip Wheelwright, "Eliot's Philosophical Themes," in *T.S. Eliot: A Study of His Writing by Several Hands*, ed. B. Rajan (London: Dennis Dobson, 1947), pp. 103-5.
4. F.O. Matthiessen, *The Achievement of T.S. Eliot*, 3rd ed. (N.Y.: Oxford University Press, 1958), p. 51.
5. Helen Gardner, *The Art of T.S. Eliot* (London: Crescent Press, 1949), p. 173.
6. Elizabeth Drew, *T.S. Eliot: The Design of His Poetry* (N.Y.: Scribner's, 1949), p. 64.
7. Kristian Smidt, *Poetry and Belief in T.S. Eliot* (Oslo: I Kommisjon Hos Jacob Dybwad, 1949), pp. 166-72.
8. Staffan Bergsten, *Time and Eternity: A Study in the Structure and Symbolism of T.S. Eliot's "Four Quartets"* (Stockholm: Svenska bokförlaget, 1960), pp. 81-84.
9. Hebert Howarth, *Notes on Some Figures behind T.S. Eliot* (Boston: Houghton Mifflin, 1964), p. 203 ff.
10. Harold McCarthy, "T.S. Eliot and Buddhism," *Philosophy East and West* 2 (1952): 31-55.
11. Narsingh Srivastava, "The Ideas of *The Bhagavad Gita* in *Four Quartets*," *Comparative Literature* 29, no. 2 (Spring 1977): 97-108.
12. Baird Shuman, "Buddhistic Overtones in Eliot's *Cocktail Party*," *Modern Language Notes* 72 (1957): 426-27.
13. Rajnath, "Whitman, Eliot, and the *Bhagavad Gita*," *Comparative Literature Studies* 20 (Spring 1983): 94-101.
14. A.G. George, *T.S. Eliot: His Mind and Art* (Bombay: Asia Publishing House, 1969), p. 48.
15. Balachandra Rajan, *The Overwhelming Question* (Toronto: University of Toronto Press, 1976), p. 10.
16. Mario Praz, *The Romantic Agony* (N.Y.: World Publishing, 1956), pp. 200-201.
17. See, for example, John Keats' *The Eve of St. Agnes*, ll. 260-65, where a number of oriental curiosities are mentioned.
18. Herbert Howarth, *Notes on Some Figures behind T.S. Eliot*, p. 203.
19. See *A Choice of Kipling's Verse*, with an Introduction by T.S. Eliot (London: Faber and Faber, 1951), p. 30.
20. *Ibid.*, pp. 23-24.
21. T.S. Eliot, "Kipling Redivivus," *Athenaeum*, (9 May 1919), pp. 297-98.
22. *A Choice of Kipling's Verse*, p. 35.
23. T.S. Eliot, *The Nation*, 158, no. 3, (15 January 1944): p. 83.
24. Rudyard Kipling, *All the Mowgli Stories* (London: Macmilan, 1952), pp. 67-81.
25. T.S. Eliot, *The Use of Poetry and the Use of Criticism* (London: Faber and Faber, 1933), p. 33.
26. *Ibid.*

27. T.S. Eliot, "Ezra Pound: A Commentary," *Criterion* 13, no. 52 (April 1934).
28. Eliot, *The Use of Poetry and the Use of Criticism*, p. 91.
29. Neville Braybrooke, "T.S. Eliot in the South Seas," in *T.S. Eliot: The Man and His Work*, ed. Allen Tate (N.Y.: Delacorte Press, 1966), pp. 387-88.
30. *Ibid.*, p. 386.
31. Kipling, *All the Mowgli Stories*, p. 122.
32. Braybrooke, "T.S. Eliot in the South Seas," p. 387.
33. Photographed from the Smith Academy Record. See *T.S. Eliot: A Symposium for His Sixtieth Birthday.*
34. Howarth, *Notes on Some Figures behind T.S. Eliot*, p. 95.
35. *Ibid.*, p. 95.
36. T.S. Eliot in his Introduction to G. Wilson Knight's *The Wheel of Fire* (London: Methuen, 1930), pp. xv-xvi.
37. T.S. Eliot, *Notes towards the Definition of Culture* (London: Faber and Faber, 1948), p. 113.
38. Howarth, *Notes on Some Figures behind T.S. Eliot*, p. 213.
39. Mario M. Rossi's comments on Yeats to Joseph Hone seem peculiarly appropriate to Eliot as well:

    Basically he did not feel philosophy as an abstract speculation nor was he attracted to it by its technical difficulties. He wanted to solve his problems. He wanted to come in clear about his own mind. He wanted to connect thing and image; to prove that the poet's expression goes further than usual vision, reaches—beyond sensation and word—the intimate transempirical nature of the world, to assure himself that the poet's way of dealing with reality is in fact a metaphysical description of it.

    See Joseph Hone's *W.B. Yeats* (N.Y.: Macmillan, 1943), p. 453.
40. See *A Source Book in Indian Philosophy*, ed. S. Radhakrishnan and Charles A. Moore (Princeton, N.J.: Princeton University Press, 1957), p. xxiii:

    Indian philosophy makes an unquestionable and extensive use of reason, but intuition is accepted as the only method through which the ultimate can be known . . . One does not merely know the philosophy, one *realizes* it. The word which most aptly describes philosophy in India is *darshana*, which comes from the ver-

bal root *drs*, meaning "to see." "To see" is to have a direct intuitive experience of the object, or rather, to realize it in the sense of becoming one with it. No complete knowledge is possible as long as there is the relationship of the subject on the one hand and the object on the other.
41. T.S. Eliot, *After Strange Gods* (N.Y.: Harcourt Brace, 1934), p. 43.
42. T.S. Eliot in a review of *Brahmadarsanam or Intuition of the Absolute*, *International Journal of Ethics* 28 (April 1918): 445-46.
43. *Ibid.*, p. 446.
44. Eliot, *After Strange Gods*, pp. 43-44.
45. Eliot, *The Use of Poetry and the Use of Criticism*, p. 91.
46. Eliot, *Notes Towards the Definition of Culture*, p. 113.
47. Eliot, *The Use of Poetry and the Use of Criticism*, p. 91. According to Stephen Spender, Eliot seriously considered becoming a Buddhist when he wrote *The Waste Land*. See Stephen Spender, "T.S. Eliot," *Encounter* (April 1965), p. 4.
48. T.S. Eliot, "Notes on *The Waste Land*" in *The Complete Poems and Plays*, p. 79.
49. Eliot, *The Use of Poetry and the Use of Criticism*, p. 95.
50. T.S. Eliot, "Dante," *Selected Essays* (London: Faber and Faber, 1958), p. 258.
51. Among the books from Eliot's library now in the Hayward Bequest in King's College Library is Vasudev Laxman Sastri Phansikar's *The Twenty-Eight Upanishads* (Bombay: Tukaram Javaji, 1906). Inscribed on the fly-leaf is the following note: Thomas Eliot with C.R. Lanman's kindest regards and best wishes. Harvard College, May 6, 1912. See Helen Gardner, *The Composition of the "Four Quartets"* (London: Faber and Faber, 1978), p. 54.
52. Eliot, "Notes on *The Waste Land*," *The Complete Poems and Plays*, p. 79.
53. *Ibid.*
54. *Ibid.*, p. 80.
55. *Ibid.*
56. H.C. Warren, *Buddhism in Translations* (N.Y.: Atheneum, 1963), p. 109.
57. The term "Vedanta" literally means "the end of the Vedas," those Hindu scriptures which are the most ancient religious writings now known in the world. Within the Indian philosophical tradition, the term Vedanta is applied primarily to the teachings of the Upanishads, the *Brahma-sutras*, and the *Bhagavad Gita*. Generally speaking,

the term Vedanta covers not only the teachings of these primary texts, but also the whole body of literature which explains, elaborates, and comments upon them. Among the different interpretations of the primary texts, the non-dualistic system of Vedanta expounded primarily by Sankara (c. 788-820 A.D.) has been, and continues to be, the most widely accepted system of thought among Indian philosophers. By common consent, it is one of the greatest philosophical achievements to be found

in the East or the West.

The term Buddhism primarily applies to the teachings of the Buddha (563-483 B.C.). In later times, after the Buddha's death, the Hinayana and the Mahayana Schools of Buddhism came into being.

I have used the Upanishads, the *Gita*, the works of Sankara, the Sermons of the Buddha, and *The Dhammapada* in this exposition.

58. Eliot, Introduction to *The Wheel of Fire*, p. xiii.

NOTES TO CHAPTER ONE

1. Cf. Kristian Smidt, *Poetry and Belief in the Work of T.S. Eliot* (Oslo: I Kommisjon hos Jacob Dybwad, 1949), p. 166:
   Just as Eliot's interest in Western philosophy can still clearly be traced in his poetry, so his study of Oriental philosophies and religions have left indelible marks. It is not always easy to distinguish these marks from those left by Christian mysticism, and one risks attaching too much importance to concrete references such as the quotation from *The Bhagavad Gita* in "The Dry Salvages." There are obvious points of contact between Eastern and Western thought. The two currents meet in the New Testament, while in the Old Testament, which has become a part of the basis of Western culture, we really meet a tributary of the Oriental tradition. Thus, *Ecclesiastes*, which Eliot draws upon constantly, presents a view of life related to that of Buddhism. If, however, the distinctions of Eastern and Western mysticism are not always easy to draw, Eliot's allusions show at least that he has often had the Oriental mystics in mind. . . . *These allusions call our attention to a far profounder saturation of Eliot's poetry with Hindu and Buddhist thought than they immediately indicate.* (my emphasis)

2. *The Bhagavad Gita*, tr. by Juan Mascaro (Harmondsworth: Penguin, 1962), p. 49.

3. From the Anguttara-nikaya iii, 134, in H.C. Warren's *Buddhism in Translations*.

4. Greatly simplified, the Vedantic and Buddhist argument runs thus: All things eventually pass away. On account of our fragility, we are susceptible to disease and death. Our hopes, our wishes, our desires, our ambitions, our personalities—all of them

will be forgotten as if they had never existed. This is a universal phenomenon. Nothing abides forever, everything changes and perishes. If we crave what changes and perishes, therefore, our desires are never satisfied and we are full of suffering. It is the impermanence of the object of our craving that causes disappointment and sorrow. Hence, suffering and impermanence are virtually one and the same.

5. T.S. Eliot, "Dante," *Selected Essays* (London: Faber and Faber, 1958), p. 275.

6. The idea that the phenomenal world is in a constant state of flux is present in Heraclitus. But Heraclitus does not specifically associate flux or impermanence with suffering. Also, as Elizabeth Drew has pointed out in her book, *T.S. Eliot: The Design of His Poetry* (N.Y.: Scribner's, 1949), p. 148, Heraclitus has no concept of a "still point" where there is "neither arrest nor movement" (BN, p. 173).

7. E.M. Forster, "T.S. Eliot," *Abinger Harvest* (London: Edward Arnold, 1965), p. 112.

8. Charles Baudelaire, "Fusées," *Journaux intimes: Oeuvres complètes* (Pléiade, 1961), p. 1263.

9. Even Eliot's admirers disagree over the qualities for which the poem should be admired. Edmund Wilson speaks of it, in *Axel's Castle* (N.Y.: Scribner's, 1931), pp. 105-14, as "simply one triumph after another," but understands it essentially as a statement of despair and disillusionment. Helen Gardner maintains that it is actually "an *Inferno* which looked towards *Purgatario*" and perhaps a *Paradiso*, in her book, *The Art of T.S. Eliot* (N.Y.: Dutton, 1959), p. 98. Critical of both these

views, I.A. Richards argues that *The Waste Land* is a poem effecting "a complete severance between ... poetry and all beliefs," in "The Poetry of T.S. Eliot," *Principles of Literary Criticism* (N.Y.: Harcourt, Brace and World, 1934), pp. 290-92. Neither Cleanth Brooks nor Norman Nicholson has interpreted *The Waste Land* satisfactorily. They interpret it as a poem of Christian faith rather than of intense suffering and hope, which are universal.

10. Cf. Herbert Howarth, *Notes on Some Figures behind T.S. Eliot* (Boston: Houghton Mifflin, 1964), pp. 234-37:

In the summer of 1921, Eliot saw *Le Sacre du Printemps* in London....Its music, he told the *Dial,* metamorphosed the "rhythm of the steppes" into the scream of the motor horn, the rattle of machinery, the grind of wheels, the beating of iron and steel, the roar of the underground railway and the other barbaric cries of modern life. It brought home the continuity of the human predicament: primitive man on the dolorous steppes, modern man in the city with its "despairing noises"; the mind of the one a continuation of the mind of the other, the essential problem unchanging. Eliot's interpretation of Stravinsky suggests that a theme of *The Waste Land* is *the unchanging predicament of man, and the unchanging remedy.* (my emphasis)

11. Eliot, "Thoughts after Lambeth," *Selected Essays,* p. 368.

12. T.S. Eliot in his Introduction to Djuna Barnes' *Nightwood* (London: Faber and Faber, 1936), p.5.

13. T.S. Eliot, *The Waste Land,* a facsimile and transcript of the original drafts including the annotations of Ezra Pound, ed. Valerie Eliot (London: Faber and Faber, 1971), p. 3.

14. Tiresias is a celebrated seer of ancient Greek mythology. His name means that he is "a seeker of signs." He comes across coupling snakes, strikes them with his staff, and is transformed into a woman for seven years. At the end of this period, he again encounters the two snakes coupling, strikes them, and regains his male form. The other signal event in his life is the loss of his eyesight as a punishment for seeing Pallas Athene bathing in the nude. As a consequence of his peccadilloes, Tiresias is a blind hermaphrodite, gifted with fore-knowledge. He resembles the Hindu figure *Ardhanārisvara,* probably the best known of the Eastern hermaphroditic deities—a fused embodiment of the male and female principles of the universe, of *Siva* and his *Sakti.*

15. Stephen Spender, "T.S. Eliot," *Encounter* (April 1965), p. 4.

16. Critics like Grover Smith and D.W. Harding do acknowledge the fact that Tiresias "sees the substance of the poem." But they are at a loss to explain how Tiresias can see both ancient and modern lives at once, or how the past and present can co-exist in his consciousness in such rich detail. And how can he possibly sense the trials and tribulations of a wide range of characters, so different from each other in terms of historical setting, social status and culture? If, on the other hand, we discard or underplay Tiresias' role in the poem, as Ian Hamilton and Graham Martin are inclined to do, the poem falls apart, losing all coherence and unity. It is only when we perceive that Tiresias is *reliving* his past lives in "every detail of desire, temptation and surrender" (like Kurtz) that we recognize the crucial role he plays in the poem. His consciousness is all-inclusive precisely because he has gained a measure of self-confidence through suffering in several lives.

17. Drew, *T.S. Eliot: The Design of His Poetry,* pp. 85-86.

18. Joyce uses metempsychosis as a motif in *Ulysses,* a work which Eliot admired and wished to emulate. Indeed, metempsychosis seems to be at the bottom of Eliot's constant view of human beings metamorphosed in the most curious ways:
And I must borrow every changing shape
To find expression ... dance, dance
Like a dancing bear,
Cry like a parrot, chatter like an ape.
(PL, p. 21)
Prufrock imagines himself to be a crab, Tiresias assumes a number of different identities, and the Hollow Men are reduced to being scarecrows.

19. Jessie L. Weston, *From Ritual to Romance* (N.Y.: Doubleday Anchor Books, 1957), p. 26.

20. *Ibid.,* p. 32.

21. *Ibid.* p. 32.

22. *Ibid.,* p. 203.

23. *Ibid.,* p. 125.

24. *Ibid.,* p. 126.
25. *Ibid.,* p. 150.
26. See John B. Vickery, *The Literary Impact of "The Golden Bough"* (Princeton, N.J.: Princeton University Press, 1973), pp. 236-61.
27. *Ibid.,* p. 261. See also Jessie Weston's *From Ritual to Romance,* p. 204.
28. Vickery, *The Literary Impact of "The Golden Bough, "* p. 261.
29. *Ibid.,* p. 248.
30. *Ibid.*
31. Others besides Eliot were conscious of *ennui* and the acute suffering it entails. For instance, Paul Valéry makes his Socrates allude to "that evil amongst all evils, that poison of poisons, that venom inimical to all nature" in *L'Ame et la danse.* See Paul Valéry, *Dialogues,* tr. by William McCausland Stewart (N.Y.: Pantheon, 1956), p. 51.
32. For a lucid explanation of the term *karma,* see *The Bhagavad Gita,* tr. by Eliot Deutsch (N.Y.: Holt, Rinehart and Winston, 1968), p. 12: The term *karma* means "deed," "work," "action," and is used in the Hindu tradition to mean both any action which produces tendencies or impressions *(sanskaras)* in the actor, which then function as determinants to his future action, and specific ritual actions which are performed in the context of Vedic ceremonial religion. Further, according to most of the Indian philosophical systems, *karma* suggests a "law" of moral nature which holds that actions necessarily produce effects and that this is enacted over a period of innumerable birth, deaths and rebirths. Every action must produce its results—if not immediately, then at some future time— and every disposition to act is the result of one's past action. One is completely responsible for oneself. A man's present condition is the result of his past action over many lives, and his future condition will result from his past and present action.

NOTES TO CHAPTER TWO

1. *The Bhagavad Gita,* tr. Juan Mascaro (Harmondsworth: Penguin, 1962), p. 101.
2. H.C. Warren, *Buddhism in Translations* (N.Y.: Atheneum, 1963), pp. 175-79.
3. W.R. Inge, *The Platonic Tradition in English Religious Thought* ((London: Routledge and Kegan Paul, 1926), p. 8.
4. *The Holy Bible,* ed. by Herbert G. May and Bruce M. Metzer (N.Y.: Oxford University Press, 1962), p. 1469.
5. According to the Neo-Platonist, Hans Leisegang, the symbol of the wheel is implicit in *Timaeus.* See Hans Leisegang, *Die Begriffe der Zeit and Ewigkeit in späteren Platonismus* (Muenster, 1913), p. 4.
6. See J.E. Circlot's *A Dictionary of Symbols* (London: Routledge and Kegan Paul, 1967), p. 371.
7. *King Lear* IV. vii. 46-48.
8. *The Poems of John Donne,* ed. by H. Grierson (London: Oxford University Press, 1949), p. 239.
9. T.E. Hulme, *Speculations: Essays in Humanism and the Philosophy of Art* (London: Routledge and Kegan Paul, 1936), p. 34.
10. Inge, *The Platonic Tradition in English Religious Thought,* p. 8.
11. Herbert Howarth, *Notes on Some Figures behind T.S. Eliot,* pp. 204-5. See also Introduction, note 47.
12. T.S. Eliot, *The Waste Land,* a facsimile and transcript of the original drafts including the annotations of Ezra Pound, ed. Valerie Eliot (London: Faber and Faber, 1971), p. 31.
13. *Ibid.,* p. 105.
14. *Ibid.*
15. Philip Wheelwright, "Eliot's Philosophical Themes," in *T.S. Eliot: A Study of His Writings by Several hands,* ed. B. Rajan (London: Dennis Dobson, 1947), p. 104.
16. The idea is that every living creature undergoes a number of deaths and rebirths until it attains perfection. And when a human being has liberated himself, not only from all earthly desires, but also from the delusion that the world of senses has any real existence, then his true Self *(Atman)* finds its identity with the Absolute *(Brahman).* This is the final aim of all meditation, the end of Yoga. For those who do not attain the ultimate goal, there is no escape from the cycle of perpetual rebirths, nor is there any hope for them to be born into a world that has made some

positive progress since they were last born. They are, in fact, bound to the Wheel of Existence or *saṁsāra;* propelled along the circumference of the wheel, they are unaware of the timeless centre, God.

17. Eliot seems to use the notion of metempsychosis literally and metaphorically. In the final published version of *The Waste Land,* the symbolic significance of the 'fall' from a higher to a lower incarnation and the 'rise' from a lower to a higher incarnation seems predominant. However, from the manuscripts of *The Waste Land,* it is quite clear that Eliot was well aware of the literal and religious implications of metempsychosis.

18. Eliot, *The Waste Land,* a facsimile and transcript, p. 105.

19. Rudyard Kipling, *Kim* (N.Y.: Scribner's, 1913), p. 346.

20. Critics of Eliot fall chiefly into two camps, one taking his note on Tiresias seriously and the other discarding it as unimportant. Grover Smith best exemplifies the former camp, while Hugh Kenner and Ian Hamilton represent the latter. Smith accepts as axiomatic that within the maze of Tiresias' consciousness alone can the various characters commingle. But he is well aware that in the world of past actions Tiresias and the characters are distinct from each other and that "there must be a difference between the perceiver and the perceived, imposed by time if nothing else" (see Grover Smith's *T.S. Eliot's Poetry and Plays: A Study of Sources and Meaning* [Chicago: University of Chicago Press, 1956], p. 68). In other words, Tiresias is the spectator, and the other characters are the actors on the stage of his consciousness. How can Tiresias possibly know all these *personae* and their actions, separated as they are by time and distance, *in such intimate detail?* Smith and his followers glide over this difficulty and busy themselves with the unearthing of the sources of Eliot's numerous quotations. Kenner and his followers ignore Eliot's note altogether and quite arbitrarily assume that there is no single protagonist or point of view in the poem. They run the risk, therefore, of explicating a poem which does not internally cohere, a poem which disintegrates into several smaller poems and a meaningless jumble of quotations. Also, they are at a loss to explain why Eliot includes so many characters and episodes illustrating the same pattern of sensual craving, gratification, and suffering.

Tiresias is no doubt the spectator. But the characters are not totally distinct from his personality. He has been all those characters and enacted their different lives, at one stage or another, in his long journey towards the freedom of *nirvāṇa,* or the peace that passes understanding. With his refined consciousness, he can now *contain* them all in his gnostic vision and grasp how his own past deeds have determined the nature of his subsequent lives and actions. (In fact, his understanding is very similar to that of Arjuna in the *Gita,* who realizes that his own past deeds have brought him to the battlefield.) In other words, all the characters in the poem are stages in his quest towards *Brahman;* this is why he knows them and their actions so intimately. In Hindu-Buddhist terms, his own *karma* has ruled over all the different incarnations of Tiresias; this is why there are so many different characters and episodes illustrating the same pattern of impulse, action and suffering. And theoretically, it is possible for Tiresias' consciousness to include many more characters. The manuscripts of *The Waste Land* do indicate that Eliot toyed with the idea of including many other 'incarnations,' but refrained from doing so because of Pound's disapproval. *The Waste land,* in fact, is a marvellously open-ended poem, capable of infinitely expanding the consciousness of its readers, and making them aware of existential realities outside and beyond the poem. Matthiessen quotes from one of Eliot's unpublished lectures a comment on the necessity of writing poetry "without a shadow of a lie":

> This speaks to me of that at which I have long aimed, in writing poetry; to write poetry which should be essentially poetry, with nothing unpoetic about it, poetry standing naked in its bare bones, or poetry so transparent that we should not see the poetry, but that which we are meant to see through the poetry, poetry so transparent that in reading it we are intent on what the poem points at, and not on the poetry, this seems to be the thing to try for. To get beyond poetry, as Beethoven, in his later works, strove to get beyond music. We never succeed, perhaps.

See Matthiessen, *The Achievement of T.S. Eliot: An Essay on the Nature of Poetry,* 3d ed. (N.Y.: Oxford University Press, 1959), p. 90.

21. Eliot, *The Waste Land,* a facsimile and transcript, p. 121.
22. *Ibid.,* p. 41.
23. *Ibid.* p. 41
24. *Ibid.,* p. 59.
25. Eliot, *The Complete Poems and Plays,* p. 60.
26. Wallace Stevens, "Two or Three Ideas," *Opus Posthumous* (N.Y.: Knopf, 1957), p. 203.
27. *The Waste Land,* a facsimile and transcript, p. 92.
28. *Ibid.,* p. 97.
29. *Ibid.,* p. 93.
30. *Ibid.,* p. 97.
31. *Ibid.,* p. 93.
32. *Ibid.,* p. 97.
33. The seventeenth century in English Literature, Eliot's chief source of literary inspiration next to Dante, is characterized by an acute awareness of the the transience of life and the tyranny of time. The medieval figures of Time and Death make their reappearance in art and literature at the end of the Renaissance, and Time has been called "the uncanny goddess of the Baroque." Essential to the Baroque mind is its love of contrasts and antitheses, and against the transience of the temporal world is set the stillness of eternity. Naturally, the eternal dimension is emphasized in particular by the religious poets, as in Vaughan's poem on the vision of eternity. The triumph of eternity over time and death is affirmed again and again in Donne's *Holy Sonnets.* And Marvell ironically speaks of the approach of "Time's winged chariot." Thus, seventeenth-century English literature may have stimulated Eliot to metaphysical speculation on time and eternity.
34. *The Bhagavad Gita,* tr. Juan Mascaro, p. 52.
35. Thomas Kyd, *The Spanish Tragedy,* in *Elizabethan and Stuart Plays,* ed. Charles Read Baskerville, et al. (N.Y.: Harcourt, Brace, 1934), IV: i.
36. Joel 2: 12-13.
37. Cited by Duncan Jones, "Ash Wednesday," in *T.S. Eliot: A Study of His Writings by Several Hands,* p. 40.
38. See Smith, *T.S. Eliot's Poetry and Plays,* p. 261.
39. See *The Bhagavad Gita,* tr. Juan Mascaro, pp. 50, 55, 67.
40. *The Portable Emerson* (N.Y.: Viking, 1946), p. 343.
41. See W.B. Yeats, *Essays and Introductions* (London: Macmillan, 1961), p. 465. Yeats is quoting Vaughan.
42. *King Lear* IV. vii. 46-48.
43. Dante, *Paradiso,* ed. H. Oelsner, with a translation by Philip H. Wicksteed (Dent, 1899), XXXIII, 142-45. St. Augustine, *Confessions,* English translation by W. Watts (London, 1946), VIII, 5: 10.
44. Edwin Arnold, *The Light of Asia* (London: Routledge and Kegan Paul, 1954), p. 139. Eliot read *The Light of Asia* as a boy, and its epic delineation of the noble and compassionate life of the Buddha left a vivid and lasting impression on his mind. Much later in his life, he nostalgically recalled the experience: "I must have had a latent sympathy for the subject matter, for I read it through with gusto, and more than once." See T.S. Eliot, "What is Minor Poetry?" in *On Poetry and Poets* (N.Y.: Noonday Press, 1961), p. 38.
45. T.S. Eliot, in his Introduction to Djuna Barnes' *Nightwood (London: Faber and Faber, 1936),* p. 5.

NOTES TO CHAPTER THREE

1. *The Bhagavad Gita,* tr. Juan Mascaro (Harmondsworth: Penguin, 1962), p. 59.
2. W. Rahula, *What the Buddha Taught* (Bedford: Gordon Fraser, 1967), p. 108.
3. Grover Smith, *T.S. Eliot's Poetry and Plays: A Study in Sources and Meaning* (Chicago: University of Chicago Press,1956), p. 14.
4. *The Norton Introduction to Literature,* ed. Carl E. Bain, Jerome Beaty, and J. Paul Hunter, 2d ed. (N.Y.: Norton, 1977), p. 730.
5. Smith, *T.S. Eliot's Poetry and Plays,* p. 107.
6. *The Upanishads,* tr. Juan Mascaro (Harmondsworth: Penguin, 1965), pp. 91-92.
7. *The Bhagavad Gita,* tr. by Swami Prabhavananda and Christopher Isherwood (N.Y.: New American Library, 1954), p. 80.
8. *Shankara's Crest-Jewel of Discrimination,* tr. by Swami Prabhavananda and Christopher Isherwood (Hollywood, Cal.: Vedanta Press, 1953), pp. 14-15.
9. *Ibid.,* p. 68.
10. Staffan Bergsten, *Time and Eternity: A Study in the Structure and Symbolism of T.S. Eliot's "Four Quartets"* (Stockholm: Svenska bokförlaget, 1960), p. 101.
11. F.H. Bradley, *Appearance and Reality* (London: Sonnenschein, 1893), p. 9.
12. *Ibid.,* p. 432.
13. *Ibid.,* p. 453.
14. *Ibid.,* p. 140.
15. A quite convincing case may be made out for seeing even Prufrock as foreshadowing the appearance of Tiresias in Eliot's poetry. Prufrock compares himself to "Lazarus . . . come back from the dead" (LP, p. 16) and, at one point in his agitated reverie, declares that he should have been a crab; later, he claims to have seen his own "head . . . brought in upon a platter" (LP, p. 15). It would seem, therefore, that Prufrock, like Tiresias, experiences several lives simultaneously.
16. T.S. Eliot, *The Waste Land,* a facsimile and transcript, ed. Valerie Eliot (London: Faber and Faber, 1971), p. 3.

17. *The Teachings of Bhagvan Sri Ramana Maharishi,* ed. Arthur Osborne (London: Rider, 1962), p. 10.
18. Christmas Humphreys, *Buddhism* (Harmondsworth: Penguin, 1951), p. 82. Eliot refers us in his notes (*WL,* p. 79) to a quotation from Hermann Hesse's *Blick ins Chaos,* describing a similar phenomenon: "Ueber diese Lieder lacht der Bürger beleidigt, der Heilige und Seher hört sie mit Tränen." Hesse was deeply influenced by Indian philosophy; he was especially captivated by Buddhism. He embodied certain basic Indian philosophical themes in his book *Siddhartha.* Siddhartha was the original name of the Buddha before he became enlightened. In *Siddhartha,* the name belongs to the protagonist who encounters the Buddha.
19. Cf. *Aphorisms of Yoga by Bhagwan Shree Patanjali,* done into English from the original in Sanskrit with a commentary by Shree Purohit Swami and an introduction by W.B. Yeats (London: Faber and Faber, 1936), p. 62:

    The forces of attachment and detachment simulataneously work on the mind, a constant fight goes on between worldly pleasures and spiritual pleasures; with the help of spiritual pleasures the yogi controls the worldly pleasures, with the help of renunciation he controls the spiritual pleasures, till he attains the seedless Samadhi.

20. Matthew Arnold, "Stanzas from the Grande Chartreuse," *The Portable Matthew Arnold* (N.Y.: Viking, 1960), p. 151.
21. Cf. "Little Gidding," *Four Quartets,* p. 195:

    > See, now they vanish,
    > The faces and the places, with the self
    > which, as it could, loved them,
    > To become renewed, transfigured,
    > in another pattern.

22. Cf. "The Dry Salvages," p. 180: "So the darkness shall be the light, and the stillness the dancing."
23. T.S. Eliot, *Elizabethan Essays* (London: Faber and Faber, 1934), pp. 189-90.
24. *Ibid.,* p. 194.

NOTES TO CHAPTER FOUR

1. T.S. Eliot in Introduction to Djuna Barnes' *Nightwood* (London: Faber and Faber, 1936), p. 5.
2. Indian philosophical and mystical disciplines from the Upanishads to the contemporary TM (Transcendental Meditation) have but one object: the penetration into the self of man, to the timeless centre of the wheel of existence, the end of rebirth and suffering. This penetration can take place at any moment; salvation is a perpetual possibility independent of historical events.
3. Cf. T.S. Eliot, *Criterion* 4, no. 1 (Jan. 1926): 5:

   Art reflects the transitory as well as the permanent condition of the soul; we cannot wholly measure the present by what the past has been, nor by what we think the future ought to be.
4. *The Bhagavad Gita,* tr. Juan Mascaro (Harmondsworth: Penguin, 1962), p. 106.
5. "Udana 8," *The Minor Anthologies of the Pali Canon,* Part II, tr. F.L. Woodward (London: Oxford University Press, 1935), p. 97.
6. *The Upanishads,* tr. F. Max Müller (N.Y.: Dover Publications, 1962), pp. 137-38.
7. "Udana 80-81," *Buddhist Texts through the Ages,* ed. Edward Conze (Oxford: Bruno Cassirer, 1954), p. 95.
8. Rudyard Kipling, *Kim* (N.Y.: Doubleday, 1901), p. 258.
9. Arthur Schopenhauer, *The World as Will and Idea* (London: Paul, Trench, Trübner, 1907), II:528.
10. T.S. Eliot, *After Strange Gods* (N.Y.: Harcourt, Brace, 1934), p. 43.
11. Audrey F. Cahill, *T.S. Eliot and the Human Predicament* (Pietermaritzburg: University of Natal Press, 1967), pp. 58-59.
12. J.E. Circlot, *A Dictionary of Symbols* (London: Routledge and Kegan Paul, 1967), p. 275.
13. *Dictionary of Symbols and Imagery* (London: North Holland Publishing, 1974), p. 305.
14. For a detailed discussion, see Ajit Mookerjee and Madhu Khanna, *The Tantric Way* (London: Thames and Hudson, 1977), pp. 66-69.
15. *The Bhagavad Gita,* tr. Juan Mascaro, p. 54.

16. Anada Coomaraswamy, *The Dance of Siva: Fourteen Indian Essays* (N.Y.: Sunwise Turn, 1918), p. 65.
17. It is interesting to compare Valéry's conception of the dance as a liberating force with Eliot's collocation of "the still point" and the "dance." According to Valéry's Socrates in *L'Ame et la danse,* the dance is a poem: "this world of exact forces and studied illusions" represents the mind in movement. It is, says Socrates, the mysterious movement of life itself transformed into a dancing girl, "making what is divine in a mortal woman shine before our eyes." He continues as if inspired by the very ecstasy of the dancer:

    She turns, and all that is visible detaches itself from the soul, all the slime of her soul is separated at the last from its most pure; men and things will form around her a shapeless whirl . . .
    She would rest motionless in the very center of her movement. Alone, alone to herself, like the axis of the world.

    Socrates argues that the poet, like the dancer, may attain complete possession of his Self and reach a pitch of perfection which can only be momentarily recaptured. Thus, poetry gives us the power to "penetrate into another world," just like the dance. And the last words of the dancer, as of the poet, are: "O Whirlwind! I was in thee, O Movement—outside all things" (see Paul Valéry, *Dialogues,* tr. William McCausland Stewart [N.Y.: Pantheon Books, 1956], pp. 57-62).
    Eliot knew Valéry's work. He wrote an introduction to Valéry's *The Art of Poetry,* translated from the French by Denise Folliot. He also wrote a critique on Valéry's works in his book, *From Poe to Valéry.*

    Eliot and Valéry were not the only ones to be fascinated with the dance. Yeats used the symbol of the dance in "Among School Children" and "Byzantium":

    How can we tell the dancer
    from the dance?

And all complexities of fury
    leave,
Dying into a dance,
An agony of trance,
An agony of flame that cannot
    singe a sleeve.

And Rilke used the symbol of the dance in a manner that closely resembled Valéry's:

As in the hand a match glows, swiftly white before it bursts in flame and to all sides licks its quivering tongues: within the ring of spectators her wheeling dance is bright, nimble, fervid, twitches and grows wide. And suddenly is made of pure fire.

(*Rainer Maria Rilke: Fifty Selected Poems with English Translations*, tr. C.F. MacIntyre [Berkeley: University of California Press, 1941], p. 87.)

18. *The Bhagavad Gita*, tr. Juan Mascaro, p. 54. See also Shree Purohit Swami, *The Ten Principal Upanishads* (London: Faber and Faber, 1970), p. 92.
19. Mookerjee and Khanna, *The Tantric Way*, p. 68.
20. Herbert V. Guenther, *The Tantric View of Life* (London: Shambala Publications, 1972), pp. 82-83.
21. Mookerjee and Khanna, *The Tantric Way*, p. 62.
22. *Ibid.*, pp. 64-66.
23. T.S. Eliot, "Choruses from *The Rock*," *The Complete Poems and Plays*, p. 160:

And the men who turned towards
    the light and were known of the
    light
Invented the Higher Religions; and
    the Higher Religions were good
And led men from light to light.

Revelation through an Incarnation is not a unique event in Hindu thought as it is in Christianity. However, nowhere in Hindu philosophical literature is revelation through an Incarnation depicted so magnificently as in *The Bhagavad Gita*. Indeed, as a poem of Annunciation, it is unparalleled. It is, therefore, quite natural for Eliot to allude to the *Gita* in dealing with the Annunciation in "The Dry Salvages." He seems to have assimilated the teachings of the *Gita* to the point of producing them as his own.

24. *The Bhagavad Gita*, tr. and ed. Swami Jagadishwarananda and Swami Jagadananda (Udbodhan: Sanskrit-Bengali Edition, 1962), p. 258.
25. *The Bhagavad Gita*, tr. Eliot Deutsch (N.Y.: Holt, Rinehart and Winston, 1968), p. 74.
26. *The Dhammapada* (Harmondsworth: Penguin, 1973), p. 89.
27. *Pali-English Dictionary* (Colombo: Pali Text Society, 1954), p. 154.
28. See *Buddhism*, ed. Richard A. Gard (N.Y.: George Braziller, 1962), p. 71: "The compound word *Tathagata* may be broken up as *Tatha (there)* + *Gata* (gone), or as *Tatha* (there) + *Gata* (arrived)."
29. *Ibid*, p. 71.
30. See *The Bhagavad Gita*, tr. Juan Mascaro, p. 53: "When thy mind leaves behind its dark forest of delusion, thou shalt go beyond the scriptures of times past and still to come." See Shankara's *Crest-Jewel of Discrimination*, tr. Swami Prabhavananda and Christopher Isherwood (N.Y.: New American Library, 1970), p. 40: "Scorched by the fierce flames of the world-forest, the disciple speaks these words. The great soul looks at the disciple who thus seeks refuge in him, and his eyes are wet with tears of mercy. Immediately, he frees his disciple from his fear."
31. See Baird Shuman's "Buddhistic Overtones in Eliot's *Cocktail Party*," *Modern Language Notes* 72 (1957): 426-27, for an example of gross misinterpretation. Shuman accepts as a fact that Eliot was influenced by Buddhism and sees attributes of a Buddhist monk in Celia. He comments: "Following Reilly's advice to 'work out your salvation with diligence,' she proceeds to do so by implicitly subscribing to the four noble truths of Buddhism. . . Her ultimate satisfaction (again according to the Buddhist rationale) is achieved in the attainment of *nirvāna*." This is incorrect. Celia does not attain *nirvāna* "according to the Buddhist rationale," which does not advocate martyrdom as a means to the realization of "the still point." Celia follows Reilly's advice no doubt, but she works out her salvation in the traditional Christian manner.
32. *The Bhagavad Gita*, tr. Juan Mascaro, p. 113.
33. H.C. Warren, *Buddhism in Translations* (N.Y.: Atheneum, 1963), p. 71.
34. *Ibid.*, p. 224.

35. *Ibid.,* p. 93.
36. *The Bhagavad Gita,* tr. Juan Mascaro, p. 92.
37. *Ibid.,* p. 59.
38. *Ibid.,* p. 62. Hindu philosophical thought and religion are basically flexible and liberal. They accept all the paths to reality shown by different seers and prophets at different times and places as equally valid. No single doctrine can be taken to be the last word, as all are essentially speculations on the unifying principle of the universe. Thus the Vedic *darśanas,* the Upanishads, the *Gita,* Patanjali's Yoga, Sankara's non-duality, Ramanuja's qualified monism, Madva's dualism, and even Buddhism and Christianity co-exist peacefully in the Hindu view of life. See Arthur Osborne's *Buddhism and Christianity in the Light of Hinduism* (London: Chatto and Windus, 1959), p. 40.
39. T.S. Eliot, *Selected Essays,* pp. 189-90.
40. Quoted by Christmas Humpreys in *Buddhism* (Harmondsworth: Penguin, 1951), p. 215.

NOTES TO THE CONCLUSION

1. There has been an increasing awareness that Eliot's works are continuous and that his individual poems must be examined in that context. See Northrop Frye, *T.S. Eliot* (Edinburgh: Oliver and Boyd, 1968), p. 49.
2. T.S. Eliot in Introduction to Djuna Barnes' *Nightwood* (London: Faber and Faber, 1936), p. 5.
3. Aldous Huxley, "The Minimum Working Hypothesis," in *Vedanta for the Western World* (N.Y.: Viking Press, 1973), p. 34.
4. Cf. "East Coker," *Four Quarters,* p. 182:

    And so *each venture*
    Is a new beginning, a raid on
      the inarticulate
    With shabby equipment always
      deteriorating
    In the general mess of imprecision
      of feeling
    Undisciplined squads of emotion.

    And what there is to conquer
    By strength and submission, has already
      been discovered
    Once or twice, or several times, by men
      whom one cannot hope
    To emulate—but there is no
      competition—
    There is only the fight to recover what has
      been lost
    And found and lost again and again: and
      now, under conditions
    That seem unpropitious. But perhaps
      neither gain nor loss,
    For us, there is only the trying. The rest is
      not our business.   (my emphasis)

5. Helen Gardner, *The Art of T.S. Eliot* (N.Y.: Dutton, 1959), p. 173.
6. Arthur Osborne, *Buddhism and Christianity in the Light of Hinduism* (London: Chatto and Windus, 1959), pp. 59-60.
7. *The Bhagavad Gita,* tr. Juan Mascaro (Harmondsworth: Penguin, 1962), p. 100.

BIBLIOGRAPHY

PRIMARY SOURCES: Works of T.S. Eliot

A. POETRY AND DRAMA

Collected Poems 1909-1962. New York: Harcourt, Brace and World, 1963.
Collected Plays. London: Faber and Faber, 1962.
The Complete Poems and Plays. London: Faber and Faber, 1969.
The Waste Land. Facsimile and transcript of the original drafts. Ed. Valerie Eliot. London: Faber and Faber, 1971.

B. PROSE

After Strange Gods: A Primer of Modern Heresy. New York: Harcourt Brace, 1934.
A Choice of Kipling's Verse. Ed. with Introduction by T.S. Eliot. London: Faber and Faber, 1951
Criterion. Ed. T.S. Eliot. 18 vols., 1922-39. London: Faber and Faber, 1967.
Elizabethan Essays. London: Faber and Faber, 1934.
Essays Ancient and Modern. London: Faber and Faber, 1936.
For Lancelot Andrewes. London: Faber and Gwyer, 1928.
From Poe to Valéry. New York: Harcourt, Brace, 1948.
"Introduction," in *The Art of Poetry* by Paul Valéry. New York: Random House, 1958.
"Introduction," in *Nightwood* by Djuna Barnes. London: Faber and Faber, 1936. Pp. 1-7.
"Introduction," in *Savonarola: A Dramatic Poem* by Charlotte C. Eliot. London: R. Cobden-Sanderson, 1926. Pp. vii-xii.
"Introduction," in *The Wheel of Fire* by G. Wilson Knight. London: Methuen, 1930. Pp. xi-xix.

"Kipling Redivivus." *Athenaeum*, 9 May 1919, pp. 297-98.
Knowledge and Experience in the Philosophy of F.H. Bradley. London: Faber and Faber, 1964.
Notes Towards the Definition of Culture. London: Faber and Faber, 1948.
"Review" of Sri Ananda Acharya's *Brahmadarsanam or Intuition of the Absolute* in *International Journal of Ethics* 28, no. 3 (April 1918): 445-46.
The Sacred Wood. London: Methuen, 1920.
Selected Essays. London: Faber and Faber, 1958.
The Use of Poetry and the Use of Criticism. London: Faber and Faber, 1933.

SECONDARY SOURCES

BIBLIOGRAPHY

Gallup, Donald. *T.S. Eliot: A Bibliography Including Contributions to Periodicals and Foreign Translations.* New York: Harcourt, Brace, 1953.
Martin, Mildred. *A Half-Century of Eliot Criticism: An Annotated Bibliography of Books and Articles in English, 1916-1965.* Lewisburg: Bucknell University Press, 1972.
The T.S. Eliot Collection. Compiled by Alexander Sacton. Austin: University of Texas, 1975.

STUDIES OF ELIOT BY ONE AUTHOR

Battenhouse, R. "Eliot's *The Family Reunion* as Christian Prophecy." *Christendom* 10 (1945): 307-21.
Bergsten, Staffan. "Illusive Allusions: Some Reflections on the Critical Approach to the Poetry of T.S. Eliot." *Orbis Litterarum* 14 (1959): 9-18.
_____. *Time and Eternity: A Study in the Stucture and Symbolism of T.S. Eliot's "Four Quartets."* Stockholm: Svenska bökforlaget, 1960.
Birje-Patil, J. *Beneath the Axle-Tree.* New Delhi: Macmillan, 1977.
Blissett, William. "The Argument of T.S. Eliot's *Four Quartets."* *University of Toronto Quarterly* 15, no. 2 (1946): 115-26.
Bolgan, Anne C. *What the Thunder Really Said: A Retrospective Essay on the Making of "The Waste Land."* Montreal: McGill-Queen's University Press, 1973.
Braybrooke, Neville. "The Boyhood of Eliot: Drawn to the South Pacific." *The Statesman,* Calcutta (India), 2 August 1970. Reprinted as "T.S. Eliot in the South Seas," in *T.S. Eliot: The Man and His Work.* Ed. Allen Tate. New York: Delacorte Press, 1966.
Brett, R.L. "Mysticism and Incarnation in the *Four Quartets.*" *English* 16 (1966): 94-99.

Cahill, A.F. *T.S. Eliot and the Human Predicament.* Mystic, Conn.: Lawrence Verry, 1967.

A Casebook: T.S. Eliot's "The Waste Land." Ed. C.B. Cox and P. Hinchliffe. London: Cohen and West, 1968.

Colby, R.A. "The Three Worlds of *The Cocktail Party:* The Wit of T.S. Eliot." *University of Toronto Quarterly* 14 (Oct. 1954): 56-69.

Drew, Elizabeth. *T.S. Eliot: The Design of His Poetry.* New York: Scribner's, 1949.

Dwivedi, Amarnath. *Indian Thought and Tradition in T.S. Eliot's Poetry.* Bareilly: Prakash Book Depot, 1977.

Fowler, Russell T. "Krishna and the 'Still Point': A Study of *The Bhagavad Gita's* Influence on Eliot's *Four Quartets." Sewanee Review* 79 (1971): 407-23.

Frye, Northrop. *T.S. Eliot.* Rev. ed. Edinburgh: Oliver and Boyd, 1968.

Gardner, Helen. *The Art of T.S. Eliot.* New York: Dutton, 1959.

George, A.G. *T.S. Eliot: His Mind and Art.* 2d rev. ed. New York: Asia Publishing House, 1969.

Greene, E.J.H. *T.S.Eliot et la France.* Paris: Boivin, 1951.

Hamalian, Leo. "Wishwood Revisited." *Renascence* 12 (1960): 167-73.

Headings, Philip R. *T.S. Eliot.* New York: Twayne, 1964.

Howarth, Herbert. *Notes on Some Figures Behind T.S. Eliot.* New York: Houghton Mifflin, 1964.

———. "T.S. Eliot's *Criterion:* The Editor and His Contributors." *Comparative Literature* 11 (1959): 97-110.

Ishak, F.M. *The Mystical Philosophy of T.S. Eliot.* New Haven, Conn.: College and University Press, 1970.

Iyengar, K.R.S. "Understanding *Four Quartets." Indian Essays in American Literature: Papers in Honour of Robert E. Spiller.* Ed. Sujit Mukherjee and D.V.K. Raghavacharyulu. Bombay: Popular Prakashan, 1969.

Jahgirdar, C.J. "T.S. Eliot's *Four Quartets: The Rhetoric of Impersonality." The Literary Criterion* 9, no. 2 (Summer 1970): 65-69.

Jones, David E. *The Plays of T.S. Eliot.* Toronto: University of Toronto Press, 1960.

Kennedy, Richard S. *Working Out Salvation with Diligence: The Plays of T.S. Eliot.* Wichita, Kan.: University of Wichita, 1964.

Kenner, Hugh. *The Invisible Poet: T.S. Eliot.* New York: McDowell Obolensky, 1959.

Krishnamurti, S. "Indian Poetics and T.S. Eliot's Three Voices of Poetry." *Half-Yearly Journal of the University of Cambridge* (New Series) 15 (1954): 15-18.

Lucy, Sean. *T.S. Eliot and the Idea of Tradition.* London: Cohen and West, 1960.

Martin, M.A. "T.S. Eliot: The Still Point and the Turning Wheel." *Bucknell Review* 4 (1953): 51-68.

Martz, Louis. "The Wheel and the Point: Aspects of Imagery and Theme in Eliot's Later Poetry." *Sewanee Review* 55 (1947): 126-47.

Matthieseen, F.O. *The Achievement of T.S. Eliot: An Essay on the Nature of Poetry.* 3d ed. New York: Oxford University Press, 1958.

Maxwell, Desmond, E.S. *The Poetry of T.S. Eliot.* London: Routledge and Kegan Paul, 1952.

Mayo, E.L. "The Influence of Ancient Hindu Thought on Walt Whitman and Eliot." *Aryan Path* 29, no. 4 (1958), 167-77.

McCarthy, Harold E. "T.S. Eliot and Buddhism." *Philosophy East and West* 2 (1952): 31-55.

Miller, Milton. "What the Thunder Meant." *English Literary History* 36 (1969): 440-54.

Misra, K.S. *The Plays of T.S. Eliot: A Critical Study.* N.Y.: Asia Publishing House, 1977.

Musgrove, Sydney. *T.S. Eliot and Walt Whitman.* Wellington, N.Z.: Wellington University Press, 1952.

Rajan, Balachandra. *The Overwhelming Question.* Toronto: University of Toronto Press, 1976.

Rajnath. "Whitman, Eliot, and the *Bhagavad Gita.*" *Comparative Literature Studies* 20 (Spring 1983): 94-101.

Ramamrutham, J.V. "T.S. Eliot and Indian Readers." *Literary Half-Yearly* 1 (1960): 46-54.

Rao, G. Nageswara. *The Epic of the Soul.* Tirupati: Sri Venkateswara University, 1977.

Rao, Narayana. "T.S. Eliot and the *Bhagavad Gita.*" *American Quarterly* 15 (1963): 572-78.

Ray, Mohit Kumar. *T.S. Eliot: Search for a Critical Credo.* Calcutta: Firma KLM Private Ltd., 1978.

Rayan, K. "Rasa and the Objective Correlative." *British Journal of Aesthetics* 5 (1965): 246-60.

Reddy, M.V. "The Concept of Time in T.S. Eliot's *Four Quartets.*" *Osmania Journal of English Studies* (1961): 31-38.

Sarkar, Subhas. *T.S. Eliot the Dramatist.* Calcutta: Minerva Associates, 1972.

Sen, S.M. *Metaphysical Tradition and T.S. Eliot.* Calcutta: Firma K.L. Mukhopadhyay, 1965.

Sharma, H. *The Essential T.S. Eliot: A Critical Analysis.* New Delhi: S. Chand, 1971.

Sharma, M.L. "The Spiritual Quest in the Poetry of T.S. Eliot." *Variations in American Literature.* Ed. Darshan Singh Maini. New Delhi: U.S. Educational Foundation in India, 1968. Pp. 26-37.

Shuman, Baird. "Buddhistic Overtones in Eliot's *Cocktail Party.*" *Modern Language Notes* 72 (1957): 426-27.

Smidt, Kristian. *Poetry and Belief in the Work of T.S. Eliot.* Oslo: I Kommisjon hos Jacob Dybwad, 1949.

Smith, Carol H. *T.S. Eliot's Dramatic Theory and Practice.* Princeton: Princeton University Press, 1963.

Smith, Grover C. *T.S. Eliot's Poetry and Plays: A Study in Sources and Meaning.* Chicago: University of Chicago Press, 1956.

Spender, Stephen. "T.S. Eliot." *Encounter,* April 1965.

Srivastava, Narsingh. "The Ideas of *Bhagavad Gita* in *Four Quartets.*" *Comparative Literature* 29, no. 2 (Spring 1977): 97-108.

Tate, Allen. *T.S. Eliot: The Man and His Work.* London: Chatto and Windus, 1967.

Thompson, Eric. *T.S. Eliot: The Metaphysical Perspective.* Carbondale: Southern Illinois University Press, 1963.

Unger, Leonard. *T.S. Eliot.* University of Minnesota Pamphlets on American Writers, No. 8.

Voskuil, Duane. "Some Philosophical Ideas in Eliot's *Four Quartets." North Dakota Quarterly* 40, no.3 (1972): 5-12.
Ward, A. "Speculations on Eliot's Time-World: An Analysis of *The Family Reunion* in Relation to Hulme and Bergson." *American Literature* 21 (1949-50): 18-34.
Weitz, M. "Time as a Mode of Salvation." *Sewanee Review* 60 (1952): 48-64.
Williams, Margaret. "T.S. Eliot and Eastern Thought." *Tamkang Review* 2, no. 1 (1971): 175-94.
Williamson, George. *A Reader's Guide to T.S. Eliot.* New York: Noonday Press, 1957.
Williamson, Hugh Ross. *The Poetry of T.S. Eliot.* New York: Putnam's, 1933.

COLLECTED ESSAYS ON ELIOT

Braybrooke, Neville, ed. *T.S. Eliot: A Symposium for His Seventieth Birthday.* New York: Farrar, Straus and Cudahy, 1958.
Kenner, Hugh, ed. *T.S. Eliot: A Collection of Critical Essays.* Englewood Cliffs, N.J.: Prentice-Hall, 1962.
Lal, P., ed. *T.S. Eliot: Homage from India. A Commemoration Volume of 55 Essays and Elegies.* Calcutta: Writer's Workshop, 1965.
March, Richard and M.J. Tambimuttu, eds. *T.S. Eliot: A Symposium for His Sixtieth Birthday.* Freeport, N.Y.: Books for Libraries Press, 1968.
Martin, Graham, ed. *Eliot in Perspective: A Symposium.* London: Macmillan, 1970.
Rajan, Balachandra, ed. *T.S. Eliot: A Study of His Writings by Several Hands.* London: Dennis Dobson, 1947.
Unger, Lenard, ed. *T.S. Eliot: A Selected Critique.* New York: Rinehart, 1948.
Wilson, Frank, ed. *Six Essays on the Development of T.S. Eliot.* London: Fortune Press, 1948.

VALUABLE ESSAYS ON ELIOT IN MORE GENERAL WORKS

Forster, E.M. "T.S. Eliot." *Abinger Harvest.* London: Edward Arnold, 1965.
Foster, Genevieve, W. "The Archetypal Imagery of T.S. Eliot." *PMLA* 60 (1945): 567-85.
Gregory, Horace and Marya Zaturenska. "T.S. Eliot, the Twentieth-Century Man of Feeling in American Poetry." *A History of American Poetry, 1900-1940.* New York: Harcourt, Brace, 1942.
Holroyd, Stuart. "T.S. Eliot." *Emergence from Chaos.* New York: Houghton Mifflin, 1957.
Leavis, F.R. "T.S. Eliot." *New Bearings in English Poetry.* London: Chatto and Windus, 1932.
Nelson, Armour H. "Critics and *The Waste Land." English Studies* 36 (1955): 1-15.
Praz, Mario. "T.S. Eliot and Dante." *The Flaming Heart.* Garden City, N.Y.: Doubleday and Co., 1956.
Unger, Leonard. "Laforgue, Conrad, and Eliot." *The Man in the Name.* Minneapolis: University of Minnesota Press, 1956.
Wilson, Edmund. "T.S. Eliot." *Axel's Castle.* New York: Scribner's, 1931.

BOOKS ON ELIOT AND OTHERS

Moorman, Charles. *Arthurian Triptych: Mythic Material in Charles Williams, C.S. Lewis, and T.S. Eliot.* Berkeley and Los Angeles: University of California Press, 1960.
Wright, G.T. *The Poet in the Poem.* Berkeley and Los Angeles: University of California Press, 1960.

INDIAN PHILOSOPHY: WORKS, EXPOSITIONS AND COMMENTARIES

HINDUISM

The Bhagavad Gita. Tr. Juan Mascaro. Harmondsworth: Penguin, 1962.
The Bhagavad Gita. Tr. Eliot Deutsch. New York: Holt, Rinehart and Winston, 1968.
―――― . Tr. Swami Jagadishwarananda and Swami Jagadananda. Udbodhan: Sanskrit-Bengali Edition, 1962.
―――― .Tr. Swami Prabhavananda and Christopher Isherwood. New York: New American Library, 1954.
Coomaraswamy, Ananda. *The Dance of Siva: Fourteen Indian Essays.* New York: Sunwise Turn, 1918.
Guenther, Herbert V. *The Tantric View of Life.* Berkeley, Cal.: Shambala Publications, 1972.
How to Know God; The Yoga Aphorisms of Patanjali. Tr. Swami Prabhavananda and Christopher Isherwood. Hollywood, Cal.: Vedanta Press, 1953.
Mookerjee, Ajit, and Madhu Khanna. *The Tantric Way.* London: Thames and Hudson, 1977.
Shankara's Crest Jewel of Discrimination. Tr. Swami Prabhavananda and Christopher Isherwood. New York: New American Library, 1970.
Swami, Purohit. *Aphorisms of Bhagwan Shree Patanjali.* Done into English from the Original in Sanskrit with a Commentary by Shree Purohit Swami and an Introduction by W.B. Yeats. London: Faber and Faber, 1936.
The Teachings of Bhagwan Sri Ramana Maharishi. Ed. Arthur Osborne. London: Rider, 1962.
The Upanishads. Tr. Juan Mascaro. Harmondsworth: Penguin, 1965.
―――― . Tr. F. Max Müller. New York: Dover Publications, 1962.

BUDDHISM

Buddhist Texts through the Ages. Ed. Edward Conze. Oxford: B. Cassirer, 1954.
The Dhammapada. Tr. Juan Mascaro. Harmondsworth: Penguin, 1973.
―――― . Tr. from the Pali with an essay on "Buddha and the Occident" by Irving Babbitt. New York: Oxford University Press, 1965.
Humphreys, Christmas. *Buddhism.* Harmondsworth: Penguin, 1951.

Osborne, Arthur. *Buddhism and Christianity in the Light of Hinduism.* London: Rider, 1959.
Pali-English Dictionary. Columbo: Pali Text Society, 1954.
Rahula, W. *What the Buddha Taught.* Bedford: Gordon Fraser, 1967.
Warren, H.C. *Buddhism in Translations.* New York: Atheneum, 1963.

INTERPRETATIONS OF INDIAN PHILOSOPHY AND CULTURE

HINDUISM

Arnold, Edwin. *The Song Celestial.* London: Routledge and Kegan Paul, 1964.
Aurobindo, Sri. *Essays on the Gita.* New York: Sri Aurobindo Library, 1950.
_____. *The Ideal of the Karmayogin.* Pondicherry: Sri Aurobindo Ashram, 1966.
_____. *The Life Divine.* 2 vols. Calcutta: Arya Publishing House, 1939-40.
_____. *The Synthesis of Yoga.* Pondicherry: Sri Aurobindo Ashram, 1965.
_____. *Thoughts and Aphorisms.* Pondicherry: Sri Aurobindo Ashram, 1968.
Bahm, A.J. *The Bhagavad Gita and the Wisdom of Krishna.* Bombay: Somaiya Publications, 1970.
Basham, A.L. *The Wonder That Was India.* New York: Taplinger Publishing Co., 1954.
Bhattacharji, S. *The Indian Theogony.* Cambridge: Cambridge University Press, 1970.
Carpenter, F.I. *Emerson and Asia.* Cambridge, Mass.: Harvard University Press, 1930.
_____. *Emerson Handbook.* New York: Hendricks House, 1953.
Cave, Sydney. *Redemption, Hindu and Christian.* London: Oxford University Press, 1919.
Coomaraswamy, Ananda. *Time and Eternity.* Ascona: Artibus Asiae, 1947.
Daniélou, Alain. *Hindu Polytheism.* London: Routledge and Kegan Paul, 1964.
Date, V.H. *Brahma-Yoga of the Gita.* New Delhi: Manoharlal, 1971.
Dechanet, J.M. *Christian Yoga.* London: Burns and Oates, 1960.
Deussen, Paul. *Outlines of Indian Philosophy.* With an appendix on the philsophy of the Vedanta in its relations to occidental metaphysics. Reprint of 1907 ed. New Delhi: Ess Ess Publications, 1976.
_____. *The Philosophy of the Upanishads.* Reprint of 1906 ed. New York: Dover Publications, 1966.
_____. *The System of the Vedanta.* Reprint of 1912 ed. New York: Dover Publications, 1973.
Deutsch, Eliot, and J.A.B. van Buitenen. *A Source Book of Advaita Vedanta.* Honolulu: University of Hawaii Press, 1971.
Devaraja, N.K. *An Introduction to Sankara's Theory of Knowledge.* New Delhi: M. Banarasidas, 1962.
Edgerton, F. *The Beginnings of Indian Philosophy.* Cambridge, Mass.: Harvard University Press, 1965.

Eliade, M. *Yoga: Immortality and Freedom*. London: Routledge and Kegan Paul, 1958.

Emerson, Ralph Waldo. *The Complete Writings*. New York: W.H. Wise, 1929.

Griffith, Ralph. *The Hymns of the Rig-Veda*. Benares: Chowkambha, 1963.

Harrison, Max H. *Hindu Monism and Pluralism*. London: Chatto and Windus, 1932.

Hopkins, E.W. *Ethics of India*. New Haven: Yale University Press, 1924.

Hume, R.E. *The Thirteen Principal Upanishads*. London: Oxford University Press, 1958.

Isherwood, Christopher. *Approach to Vedanta*. Hollywood, Cal.: Vedanta Press, 1963.

Koelman, C.M. *Patanjali Yoga*. Poona: University of Poona Press, 1970.

Krishna Prem. *The Yoga of the Bhagavad Gita*. London: Watkins, 1969.

Lanman, Charles R. *A Sanskrit Reader*. Cambridge, Mass.: Harvard University Press, 1963.

Mahadeva Sastri, A. *The Bhagavad Gita*. With the commentary by Sri Sankaracharya. Madras: R. Sastrulu, 1961.

Mahadevan, T.M.P. *Readings from Sankara*. Madras: Ganesh Press, 1960.

Mishra, U. *A Critical Study of the Bhagavad Gita*. Allahabad: Tribhukti Publications, 1954.

Müller, F. Max. *A History of Ancient Sanskrit Literature*. Rev. ed. Varanasi: Chowkhamba Sanskrit Series, 1968.

———. *India: What Can It Teach Us?* London: Longmans, Green, 1892.

———. *Introduction to the Science of Religion*. London: Longmans, Green, 1873.

———. *The Six Systems of Indian Philosophy*. London: Longmans, Green, 1919.

Müller, F. Max. *Three Lectures on Vedanta Philosphy*. 2d ed. Varanasi: Chowkhamba Sanskrit Series, 1967.

———. *The Vedas*. Calcutta: Susil Gupta, 1956.

———. *The Dhammapada*. Delhi: Banarsidas, 1881.

Nataraja Gura. *The Bhagavad Gita*. London: Asia Publishing House, 1961.

Otto, Rudolf. *Mysticism: East and West*. New York: Macmillan, 1970.

Parrinder, Geoffrey. *Avatar and Incarnation*. London: Faber and Faber, 1970.

———. *Upanishads, Gita and Bible*. New York: Association Press, 1963.

The Portable Emerson. New York: Viking Press, 1946.

The Pure Principle. An Introduction to the Philosophy of Sankara. Ed. Y. Keshava Menon and Richard F. Allen. East Lansing: Michigan State University Press, 1960.

Radhakrishnan, S. *Comparative Religion*. London: Allen and Unwin, 1933.

———. *East and West in Religion*. London: Allen and Unwin, 1954.

———. *Eastern Religions and Western Thought*. Oxford: Clarendon Press, 1940.

———. *The Hindu View of Life*. London: Allen and Unwin, 1927.

———. *A Sourcebook of Indian Philosophy*. Princeton, N.J.: Princeton University Press, 1957.

Ray, P.C. *The Mahabharatha*. Calcutta: Bharata Press, 1884.

Roy, S.C. *The Bhagavad Gita and Modern Scholarship*. London: Luzac, 1971.

Renou, Louis. *Hinduism*. New York: George Braziller, 1963.

Schlipp, Paul Arthur. *The Philosophy of Sarvepalli Radhakrishnan*. New York: Tudor Publishing Co., 1952.

Sen, K.M. *Hinduism.* Harmondsworth: Penguin, 1961.
Shankara's Brahma-Vada. Ed. R.S. Naulakha. Kanpur: Kitab Ghar, 1964.
Sharma, C. *A Critical Survey of Indian Philsophy.* London: Rider, 1960.
Shrivastava, S.N.L. *Sankara and Bradley.* New Delhi: M. Banarasidas, 1968.
Swami Jagadananda. *Upadesasahsri of Sri Sankara.* Madras: Ramakrishna Math, 1949.
Swami Nikhilananda. *Dṛg-dṛśya Viveka of Sri Sankara: An Inquiry into the Nature of the 'Seer' and the 'Seen.'* Mysore: Ramakrishna Math, 1964.
_____. *Self-Knowledge: Atma-Bodha of Sankara.* New York: Ramakrishna-Vivekananda Centre, 1946.
Swami Vivekananda. *The Complete Works.* Calcutta: Advaita Ashrama, 1963.
_____. *The Yogas and Other Works.* New York: Ramakrishna-Vivekananda Centre, 1953.
Vedanta for Modern Man. Ed. Christopher Isherwood. New York: Collier, 1962.
Vedanta for the Western World. Ed. Christopher Isherwood. London: Allen and Unwin, 1948.
What Vedanta Means to Me: A Symposium. Ed. John Yale. Garden City, N.Y.: Doubleday, 1960.
Wilson, H.H. *Rig-Veda Samhita: A Collection of Ancient Hindu Hymns.* Poona: Ashtekar, 1925.
Wood, E. *Yoga.* London: Cassell, 1959.
Woods, J.H. *Yoga-System of Patanjali.* New Delhi: Banarasidas, 1966.
Woodroffe, John. *The Serpent Power.* Madras: Ganesh Press, 1972.
Zaehner, R.C. *The Bhagavad Gita.* Oxford: Clarendon Press, 1969.

BUDDHISM

Arnold, Edwin. *The Light of Asia.* London: Routledge and Kegan Paul, 1954.
Bharati, Agehananda. *The Tantric Tradition.* London: Rider, 1965.
Bhattacharya, B. *An Introduction to Buddhist Esotericism.* 2d ed. Varanasi: Chowkhamba Sanskrit Series, 1964.
Burtt, Edwin A. *The Teaching of the Compassionate Buddha.* New York: New American Library, 1966.
Bhikshu Sangharakshita. *The Three Jewels: An Introduction to Buddhism.* London: Rider, 1966.
Conze, Edward. *Buddhism: Its Essence and Development.* Oxford: B. Cassirer, 1957.
_____. *Buddhist Thought in India.* London: Allen and Unwin, 1962.
_____. *Buddhist Wisdom Books.* London: Allen and Unwin, 1958.
Coomaraswamy, Ananda. *Buddha and the Gospel of Buddhism.* New York; Harper and Row, 1964.
Dutt, M.N. *A Prose English Translation of Mahanirvana Tantra.* Calcutta: Elysium Press, 1900.
Foucher, Alfred. *The Life of the Buddha.* Middleton, Conn.: Wesleyan University Press, 1963.
Grimm, George. *The Doctrine of the Buddha: The Religion of Reason and Meditation.* 2d rev. ed. Berlin: Akademie-Verlag, 1958.

Guenther, Herbert V. *Buddhist Philosophy in Theory and Practice.* Harmondsworth: Penguin, 1972.

Humphreys, Christmas. *The Wisdom of Buddhism.* New York: Random House, 1961.

Jayatilleke, K.N. *Early Buddhist Theory of Knowledge.* London: Allen and Unwin, 1963.

Jayatilleke, K.N. *The Message of the Buddha.* Tr. Ninian Smart. London: Allen and Unwin, 1975.

Johnston, William. *The Still Point: Reflections on Zen and Christian Mysticism.* New York: Fordham University Press, 1970.

King, W.L. *Buddhism and Christianity.* Philadelphia: Westminster Press, 1962.

Murti, T.R.V. *The Central Philosophy of Buddhism.* London: Allen and Unwin, 1960.

Nyanaponika, Thera. *The Heart of Buddhist Meditation.* London: Rider, 1962.

Parrinder, Geoffrey. *The Wisdom of the Early Buddhists.* London: Sheldon Press, 1977.

Robinson, Richard H. *The Buddhist Religion: A Historical Introduction.* London: Allen and Unwin, 1970.

Rhys Davids, T.W. *Buddhism.* London: Putnam, 1926.

Saddhatissa, H. *Buddhist Ethics.* London: Allen and Unwin, 1970.

––––––. *The Buddha's Way.* London: Allen and Unwin, 1971.

Stcherbatsky, Theodore. *Buddhist Logic.* Leningrad: Izd-Vo Akademii Nauk USSR, 1930.

Streng, Frederick J. *Emptiness: A Study in Religious Meaning.* Nashville, Tenn.: Abingdon Press, 1967.

Suzuki, D.T. *On Indian Mahayana Buddhism.* New York: Harper and Row, 1968.

Swearer, Donald. *Secrets of the Lotus: An Introduction to Buddhist Meditation.* London: Macmillan, 1971.

Thomas, Edward J. *The History of Buddhist Thought.* London: Routledge and Kegan Paul, 1968.

Welbon, Guy R. *The Buddhist Nirvana and Its Western Interpreters.* Chicago: University of Chicago Press, 1968.

Upadhyaya, K.N. *Early Buddhism and the Bhagavad Gita.* New Delhi: Banarasidas, 1971.

OTHER WORKS CONSULTED

St. Augustine. *Confessions.* With an English Translation by W. Watts. 2 vols. London: The Loeb Classical Library, 1946.

Baudelaire, Charles. *Journaux intimes, oeuvres complètes.* Pléiade, 1961.

Bradley, F.H. *Appearance and Reality.* London: Sonneschein, 1893.

Circlot, J.E. *A Dictionary of Symbols.* London: Routledge and Kegan Paul, 1967.

Dante. *Paradiso.* Ed. H. Oelsner. Translation by Philip H. Wicksteed. Dent, 1899.

Dictionary of Symbols and Imagery. London: North Holland Publishing Co., 1974.

Elizabethan and Stuart Plays. Ed. Charles Read Baskerville et al. New York: Harcourt, Brace, 1934.

The Holy Bible. Ed. Herbert G. May and Bruce M. Metzger. New York: Oxford University Press, 1962.

Hone, Joseph. *W.B. Yeats.* New York: Macmillan, 1943.

Hulme, T.E. *Speculations: Essays in Humanism and the Philosophy of Art.* London: Routledge and Kegan Paul, 1936.

Inge, W.R. *The Platonic Tradition in English Religious Thought.* London: Routledge and Kegan Paul, 1926.

Kipling, Rudyard. *All the Mowgli Stories.* London: Macmillan, 1952.

––––––. *Kim.* New York: Scribner's, 1913.

Leisegang, Hans. *Die Begriffe der Zeit und Ewigkeit in späteren Platonismus.* Muenster, 1913.

The Poems of John Donne. Ed. H. Grierson. London: Oxford University Press, 1949.

The Portable Matthew Arnold. New York: Viking Press, 1960.

Rainer Maria Rilke: Fifty Selected Poems with English Translations. Tr. C.F. MacIntyre. Berkeley: University of California Press, 1941.

Riepe, Dale. *The Philosophy of India and Its Impact on American Thought.* Springfield, Maryland: Charles C. Thomas, 1970.

Schopenhauer, Arthur. *The World as Will and Idea.* London: Paul, Trench, Trübner, 1907.

Sinclair, May. *Defence of Idealism.* London: Faber and Faber, 1917.

––––––. "Jones's Karma." *Criterion* 11, no. 45 (July 1932).

Stevens, Wallace. *Opus Posthumous.* New York: Knopf, 1957.

Valéry, Paul. *Dialogues.* Tr. William McCausland Stewart. N.Y.: Pantheon Books, 1956.

Vickery, John B. *The Literary Impact of "The Golden Bough."* Princeton, N.J.: Princeton University Press, 1973.

Weston, Jessie L. *From Ritual to Romance.* New York: Doubleday, 1957.

Yeats, W.B. *Essays and Introductions.* London: Macmillan, 1961.

INDEX